Dog Stories
©Dana Landers 2013
All Rights Reserved

Table of Contents

A Lilac Creek Dog Story

A DOG
FOR KEEPS

DANA LANDERS

A Dog for Keeps

©2012 Dana Landers

All Rights Reserved

"The dog was created especially for children. He is the god of frolic."

~Henry Ward Beecher

Chapter 1

They said it would be the winter storm to top all winter storms. The snow had begun falling around noon and in just one hour it had started to build up thick on the roads. Julia knew the plows wouldn't be out until it was all over so it was definitely time to head home. She really wished that she had left work sooner, but it had taken a while to tie up the last loose ends of her latest offer. "I guess house closings have to happen snow or not," she thought to herself as she locked the office door. She knew the Emerson couple would be grateful that the final papers were signed, but that didn't change her prospect of a long, slow drive home. Fortunately, the office wasn't far from her house and the roads would be fairly well travelled by plenty of four wheel drive vehicles heading in the same direction. If you lived in Lilac Creek, you either had to have all wheel drive for the winter or plan to hibernate for five months.

Julia hit the unlock function on her fob and welcomed the shelter from the icy wind as she got in. Sitting for a few minutes to let things warm up gave her time to start thinking ahead to the chores that would be waiting at home. With a little luck she would make it down the driveway ok, but there would be some snow removal to be done sometime over the evening. Thankfully, this was usually a shared chore with her neighbor, Sam Baxter who lived in the other half of the old house she had fallen in love with and claimed as her own over three years ago.

It was one of the oldest homes in Lilac Creek, and one of the largest. Most of the homes were more like cottages, some of them stone, but many of them painted wood or cedar sided. The duplex Julia owned had once been an Inn where many a tourist had come to stay to enjoy a respite from the hustle and bustle of city life. When the old Inn closed, a couple had tried running it as a B&B for a while, but when they decided running a business was not their passion, they sold it to a local Doctor who lived in part of the house and converted the rest to offices and examining rooms. Old Dr. McKay ran his practice there for nearly thirty years before he retired to the sunny south and put it up for sale. Julia was asked to handle the listing when it came into the office, but the paperwork never went any further than her desk. She jumped on the chance to buy the old place and had plans for its conversion to a duplex settled in her mind before the ink had dried on the last piece of paper. Now she had her own cozy, country home and an income property as well. She thanked her lucky stars every day that she had also found a fantastic tenant for the other half of the house.

Her thoughts turned now to Sam Baxter and his daughter Brinn. The tragedy that they had suffered made Julia's heart ache every time she thought about it.

Suddenly a shrill sound broke her reverie and brought her back to matters at hand. The sounds of sirens on the highway just half a mile away chilled her even more than the gloomy storm. Someone had already fallen prey to the bad roads and Julia hoped it wasn't serious. "Better get going," she thought as she pulled slowly out of the parking lot. "It's going to get a lot worse before it gets better." Julia made her way out of town with no trouble and turned onto the first country road she would have to navigate. The snow banks were already a good two feet high from previous storms. "I'll be lucky if I can see over the banks at all when this one's finished," she muttered. The snow was heavy but there was no wind so she didn't have to worry about whiteout conditions. "Slow and steady," she kept repeating to herself. "Better to make it home in one piece than in good time!" On a good day the trip from town to the tiny hamlet of Lilac Creek took about 10 minutes. In bad weather like this, it could easily take a half hour or more. The roads were winding, hilly and narrowed by encroaching snow banks. Julia crept along and within about 20 minutes she was in sight of the turn onto her road. Tire tracks leading down the road told her that Sam was likely already home. He would have most likely picked Brinn up early from the daycare she attended in town. With any luck, that would mean his heavy duty Land Rover would have made track enough in the driveway for her to get in. She looked forward to a bit of down time with a steaming cup of coffee and some supper before heading out to help with snow removal.

To her surprise, the driveway was more than just a little cleared. There was only an inch or two of snow to drive through and the walkway to her door was cleared as well. Sam was just putting the snow blower into the garage as she drove up. Brinn was playing in the snow nearby, snow gear leaving nothing exposed but the smallest bit of her face. Her bright red and yellow toque was pulled down over her ears and a matching scarf covered her mouth. Julia waved to her as she pulled carefully into her side of the garage. Sam finished wiping down the snow blower and turned in her direction. "Glad to see you headed home a little early!" He said with some surprise. Sam knew what a workaholic she was.

"Well, they said this was going to be a big one. Thought I'd get home ahead of the worst of it. Looks like you've been here for a while. Did they close the daycare early?"

Sam nodded. "I picked Brinn up a couple of hours ago. Thought I'd let her play outside for a bit while I got started on the snow."

Julia thanked him as she headed inside and promised to come out and help with the next round of clearing. "Hi sweetie," she said to Brinn as she passed by. The little girl said nothing. She glanced up from her play, and for just an instant her eyes met Julia's before turning downward once again.

Julia was still thinking about Brinn as she popped a dark roast K-Cup into her Keurig. She wished there was some way she could help. It saddened her to see a child so lost and broken, a child who should be laughing, playing and enjoying life. Instead she spent her days in silence, her voice stilled by the trauma that she no doubt relived over and over in her mind. Julia thought about how hard it had been for Sam to tell her the story. Her heart ached for him as well. She doubted there was a better father anywhere than her neighbor. She had certainly never witnessed dedication like his.

His world revolved around Brinn and his only wish in life was to hear her sweet voice once again. Julia thought back to the day they met, when he had immediately explained the tragedy.

"You should know," he had said. "If we're going to be neighbors, I want to be honest and open with you. I want you to understand why Brinn isn't like other kids." And so he had told her about the whole horrible tragedy.

Just over a year ago his wife Emily and her sister Gwen were driving home from a day of shopping. Brinn was in the back seat nestled among the day's wealth of store bought treasures. Emily had been born and raised here, in what a lot of people called "God's country." She loved the lakes, the rocks, the forests, and all the creatures that lived within their sanctuary. She was always mindful of them whenever she drove the country roads or the highway. In fact, she steadfastly refused to drive at dusk or after dark because those were the most dangerous times for animals and cars to collide. But this day it seemed, the fates had conspired against her. It was just late afternoon on a bright sunny August day when the one thing she had always feared, became her fate. She was driving carefully along the highway, watchful for wildlife that could run into the road at any moment. Unfortunately, one other driver was not so vigilant. Conditioned by years of predictable city driving, oblivious to the hazards of rural driving and travelling at a speed well above the limit, there was nothing he could do when a deer bounded out in front of his car. The high rate of speed at impact catapulted the large doe into the oncoming lane, hitting the windshield of Emily's car dead on. Emily and her sister were killed on impact. Brinn, secured in her car seat in the back was uninjured, but had to endure several traumatic minutes in the car with her Mom and Aunt before the paramedics arrived. When they arrived on the scene, Brinn was screaming hysterically for her Mommy. She was sedated and taken to hospital but released within hours. Yet, In spite of all the very best in medical treatment and counseling, she would not speak. Not even Sam's unshakable dedication and love could coax a sound from her tortured little soul.

Julia was thankful that Sam had shared the information with her. It had helped all of them form a strong and trusting friendship, one that made being good neighbors completely effortless. Julia took her cup from the hissing Keurig, added a few drops of cream and headed for the loveseat. Her plan was to enjoy her coffee and rest for a bit then bundle up to help shovel snow. Within minutes the coffee was gone and she had drifted off with her head back on the soft leather. A knock at the door startled her awake. She opened the door to a smiling Sam dressed in full outdoor attire. He had obviously finished up with the snow "I'm so sorry," she said. I must have drifted off.

"No worries," said Sam. "The snow stopped about a half hour ago. We're all good. Should ne no trouble getting out in the morning."

"Great. Thanks, and again I'm sorry." Julia closed the door, thinking once again how lucky she was to have such a great neighbor.

Chapter 2

"Blasted winter!" grumbled the old man behind the wheel of his ancient pick-up. "One of these days I'm gonna move someplace where the snow don't fall for over half the year!" The black and tan mutt riding shotgun beside him barked in agreement. Henry Thompson lived alone in the house he had built many years ago when he and Alice were happy young newlyweds. Over the years they had added a screen porch to escape the torment of black flies and mosquitoes, expanded the kitchen to include and small breakfast set, and they had just recently finished an office area where Alice could work at her writing. It had started just as a hobby, but had grown into quite a passion. Henry teased her about getting lost in her books and forgetting all about him. It wasn't true, of course, but they loved to banter back and forth. It was always friendly, never hurtful and it was apparent to everyone who knew them that they remained sweethearts even after 50 years of marriage. Most of their days were passed with simple pleasure. A bit of fishing, model building and reading for Henry and gardening, reading, and most recently writing for Alice. They asked for little from those around them but gave much to anyone who needed their help or support. They had only one child, a daughter, Wendy, who now lived in California with her husband and their three beautiful grandkids. Alice had loved those kids with every ounce of her being. She called them often, sent parcels with special surprises for every special occasion, and recently had conquered her fear of the internet and had learned to use video calling. Even though thousands of miles separated them, they were very connected. Alice's new office was the hub of all that activity and it was what Alice called her happy place. But the office pretty much sat unused these days. Henry had no desire to even step inside its cozy confines. Alice had passed away from liver cancer six months ago and her writings remained unfinished. The computer sat unopened, and little items that had been collected for mailing sat waiting. He supposed he would have to tend to all of those things someday, but that day just hadn't come yet. The day had not yet come when he would consider selling the house and maybe moving out to the coast to be near Wendy and the kids. She was always urging him to at least come for a visit, and he hadn't done that yet either. When Wendy had come home for her mother's funeral they had talked at length about what his future might hold. But he wasn't ready to do anything just yet. Most of the time, he felt like Alice was still there with him, as if he was just waiting for her to get home from some shopping trip or cooking class. He felt her presence so strongly still, that the thought of leaving felt too much like leaving her behind. He knew that time would change all that, and he was willing to let that time pass at its own speed.

For now, he had more urgent matters to deal with; this winter storm being the main one. Henry didn't usually venture out on the roads in any kind of bad weather, but he had run out of some things and wanted to get stocked up in case the storm turned out to be as big as they expected. You just couldn't trust the weather reporters to get it right. Sometimes they predicted a whopper and they ended up having flurries. And sometimes the flurries they said to expect turned into blizzards. At any rate, Henry preferred to rely on his old achy bones to tell him what was coming, and today his joints were telling him this was going to be a big one! He was pretty good at keeping his cupboards stocked during the winter, but he had been laid up for a while with a cough and fever. Now his supplies were low and another storm was hitting hard. He hunched right over top of the steering wheel and kept his eyes glued right to the road. "Keep an eye out there, Jasper, old boy," he said to the dog. "Don't want to be going off into the ditch now do we?" As if he understood exactly what the old man was saying, Jasper kept his eyes focused on some point in the distance ahead of the car. Though there was no wind to add to the poor visibility, the snow was coming down hard, creating that hypnotic effect that can be dangerous and distracting. Henry drove slowly, using the white line on his right to judge where the road was going. He was a bit disoriented and thought that they should be getting close to his driveway by now. He couldn't remember crossing the wooden bridge over Lilac Creek, or the big curve that came right afterwards. Thinking that he was maybe going a lot slower than was necessary, he decided to pick up the pace a bit, He put just a little more pressure on the gas and his old Chevy lurched forward. His thoughts were now on getting home. Suddenly out of the white whirling storm, the curve in the road that he had thought he already passed appeared, but Henry was moving too fast to take it. The truck began to fishtail. Panicking, Henry hit the brake and the truck began to slide. Instead of rounding the curve it went straight ahead, off the road and into a tree. The impact crumpled the front end and pushed the doors wide open. Jasper had been thrown to the floor when Henry hit the brakes and after a few seconds of confusion, climbed into the small crunched space that had been the front seat. His master was slumped over the twisted steering wheel. He nosed Henry's arm and whimpered. When he got no response, he started licking Henry's face. When that failed to rouse his master, he spread himself across Henry's lap. After a time, Jasper started feeling cold and thirsty. He knew there was something seriously wrong with Henry, and he knew what he had to do. Feeling a little stiff from the cramped space and his fall to the floor, Jasper crawled slowly down from the truck. He didn't know where he was but he had a sense that home was not far off. If he could find the way to his road, there were friends there who would help Henry. And so, sore and snow covered, he started out into the storm.

Chapter 3

Lilac Creek was a picture postcard the next morning. The evergreen branches wore a coat of white and the untouched snow glistened in the sunlight. Julia loved winter, especially on days like this. She enjoyed a quick breakfast of coffee and toast and dressed for the day. Real estate showings were pretty slow in January so she could spend some extra time on the marketing side of things. Once the Emerson deal closed, she'd have some time for that. Her website and brochures all needed major updates, and there were plenty of past clients to call and keep in touch with. With her mind on the day ahead, Julia headed out. Sam and Brinn were already gone and Julia was grateful for the clear driveway. She smiled to herself as she drove along, remembering what she had said to herself yesterday on the way home. "I really can't see over the snow banks!"

She saw the dog and heard the sickening thud almost simultaneously. It had run out from between two banks at the end of a driveway. There was no way she could have avoided it. Julia slowed to a stop, thankful that she had been travelling slowly on the snow packed road. Her heart was racing and her hands shaking as she got out of the car. Judging by the dark brown mound of fur, it was a pretty big dog. Warnings about confronting injured animals flashed through her head, but she knew she had to do something, and time could be crucial if the injuries were serious. She approached slowly, watchful for sudden movement or signs of aggression. What she saw instead were two large brown eyes that were entirely focused on her as she came closer. Julia didn't consider herself a dog person, and wasn't really familiar with them or their behavior, but something in this dog's eyes told her she had nothing to fear. She was totally amazed when the dog lifted his head and gave a friendly thump thump of a shaggy brown and tan tail. She didn't know dog breeds all that well but she guessed he was maybe the size of her neighbor's golden retriever, but a lot shaggier. He did have gorgeous coloring though. All black and tan and white. Some kind of a mutt, she supposed. Julia inspected the snow around the dog, elated to see no signs of bleeding. Hopefully that meant that the injuries would be minor. "Ok, great," she said to herself as much as the dog at her feet. "It seems you're not too badly hurt. But now what do I do?" As if to answer her question, she heard the hum of an approaching car. It slowed to a stop behind the dog and a young man emerged.

"Do you need some help?" he asked. Julia didn't recognize him but was grateful for his offer.

"I don't think he's badly hurt." She said. "And he seems perfectly friendly. I'd like to take him in to Dr. Westwood, if you could help me get him into my car."

"I'll give it a try," he shrugged. I've had dogs all my life, so maybe he'll know he can trust me. "Oh, I'm Travis, by the way. Travis James. I'm in town visiting my Gram. She lives over in Lilac Creek. Maybe you know her. Heddi James?"

"Sure, I know her, Julia smiled. " I found her that great little cottage last spring. I'm Julia Henderson, River Shores Real estate. Pleased to meet you." Travis bent down and stroked the dog's damp fur.

"Looks like he's somebody's pet. There's a collar but the tags have come off. He appears to be well fed, and except for some snow and ice that's caked up in his fur, he looks really healthy. Must have escaped from somewhere." Julia pondered that for a minute. She knew most of her immediate neighbors, and none of them owned a dog like this. Could belong to someone in town, or maybe even the next village down the highway. At any rate, medical attention was the most urgent matter at hand. Finding his owner could come later. In fact, Julia mused, Dr. Westwood would likely recognize him if he was from anywhere nearby. He tended to most of the animals in the area. When Travis rose, the dog struggled to get up too. He made a feeble attempt to walk, but wouldn't put any weight on his right front leg. "Could be broken," Travis said. "But I think we can get him into the car ok." Julia grabbed a blanket from the trunk of her car and spread it out on the back seat. She wasn't a neat freak or anything, but she did frequently chauffeur clients around and she was pretty sure they wouldn't appreciate dog fur on their clothes, not to mention the drool she knew was going to cover a good size portion of the small back seat. Travis helped the dog limp over to the car and then gently lifted him in. He made himself comfortable as though he rode back there every day. Julia thanked Travis for his help and they both headed off, Julia heading for the veterinary office in town and Travis heading off to visit his Gram. Julia made a mental note to tell Heddi what a remarkable grandson she had the next time she saw her.

Town was pretty quiet after yesterday's storm. No doubt everyone was still home shoveling out. Neighbors would be helping neighbors, young would be helping old, and those with snow blowers or throwers would be helping those struggling with shovels and sweat. That's what Julia really loved about small town country living. Sometimes it also meant that everybody knew your business, too, but the good definitely outweighed the bad.

She was glad to see Dr. Westwood's van parked outside the animal hospital. There were few other cars there, so she hoped that meant he didn't have patients waiting. She had tried to give him a heads up from her cell phone but he hadn't picked up. Pulling into a spot near the front door, she spoke over her shoulder to her furry passenger. "Wait here for a second. I'll be right back." She shook her head and laughed at the realization that she was talking to a dog. She'd heard many a "dog person" talk to their dog, but she never expected to hear herself doing it! She walked into the clinic and up to the counter. Even though she wasn't a pet owner and therefore not a client of the clinic, she had dealt with most of the locals seeing to their real estate needs. "Good morning, Brenda. How are you?" Brenda looked up from her computer screen and smiled.

"Hi Julia. I'm great thanks. How are you?" Julia paused for a moment before answering.

"Well, I'm fine," she said somewhat hesitantly, "but I have a passenger in my car that's not doing as well."

"Oh really?" Brenda queried. "Did you finally break down and get a pet?"

Julia laughed, "Not exactly. Actually, a rather large mutt had a run in with my car this morning. He just ran out from between two snow banks. He's not badly hurt. In fact, he walked to my car on his own. But I think he might have a broken leg." With this new information, Brenda quickly rose from her seat and headed down the short hall to the examining rooms.

"I'll get Dr. Westwood. Be right back. He'll help you bring the dog in. Just wait right there." Julia nodded. There was no need to reply. Brenda was already out of sight. Like most of the animal people she had ever met, the folks in this clinic were totally dedicated to helping and saving animals. Within seconds, Dr. Westwood appeared. Julia extended a hand.

" Morning Dr. Westwood. How are you?"

"Please call me Brent, and I'm fine. How are you doing, Julia? I understand you have a furry friend that requires attention."

"I do indeed. He's in the back seat of the car. He was a little too big for me to handle. He can walk, but I didn't have a leash."

"Let's get him in here then." Brent headed for the door with Brenda following close behind. Julia reached the car first and opened the car door as they approached. Brent leaned into the car, clipping a leash to the red collar around the dog's neck. He spoke softly to the dog as he tried to coax him onto his feet and out of the car. It didn't really take much convincing. The dog was ready to stretch and get out to relieve himself, which he did almost immediately. Julia was the only one not expecting this and almost got an unwanted shoe wash. She jumped quickly out of harm's way much to the amusement of Brenda and Brent. Meanwhile, good old doggy boy was hobbling around on three legs sniffing everything in sight.

They all trooped back inside again, this time Julia trailing behind. Julia glanced at her watch and realized she was needed in the office for a meeting with the Emersons in less than fifteen minutes. Dr. Westwood noticed her sudden concern. "I'll need a little time to examine him better," he said. "Why don't you leave him here for the day and let me have a good look at him. Maybe someone will even call looking for him." Julia thanked him for his help, and promised to return as soon as she closed up for the day. She had no appointments for showings that evening, so she promised to return before the clinic closed at 6.

"Thanks, again, Brent" Julia called over her shoulder. "See you later." As an afterthought she reached out and patted the dogs head before she left. "Good luck, big guy," she whispered. She still was quite uncomfortable with this talking to animals thing, but there was just something about those big droopy brown eyes that really got to her!

Chapter 4

Julia made it to the office with time to spare before the Emersons arrived. She got the paperwork in order and took a few minutes to refresh herself with all the details. The Emersons were relocating to Lilac Creek from the big city. They wanted a quieter, simpler life, and a better place to raise a family. They had a little boy who was almost two, and another one on the way in a few months. They were so grateful that she was able to help them find a comfortable, affordable house within walking distance to the local shops and school. They were a really nice couple, the kind of clients Julia really enjoyed. She hoped that some day she would have a life like theirs, with a loving husband, a couple of kids and ..... She chuckled as she thought of what she was about to say, And maybe a dog! Weird! Suddenly she was saving dogs, talking to dogs, and even thinking about maybe having a dog! What kind of spell was that mangy haired mutt trying to cast on her anyway? Julia shrugged.

Actually it was a lot more likely that she would have a dog in her future than a loving husband and a couple of kids, since there wasn't even a man of any sort in her life. There just weren't many eligible bachelors in the area, and she didn't exactly get out much to find any. Between fixing up the duplex and selling houses to other happy young couples, there wasn't much time left for socializing. The most contact she had with an eligible man was with Sam, and she considered him almost a best friend rather than a romantic prospect. Besides, his life was as busy as hers and she doubted if he had time for a social life either.

She heard the outer door to the office open and she stood quickly, gathering paperwork as she did. She walked into the greeting area expecting to see the Emersons and was shocked to see Sam standing there instead. It was like her thoughts had materialized right before her eyes. "Hi " she said. "I wasn't expecting to see you standing there. What's up?"

Sam smiled a little sheepishly and grinned. "I was hoping you could do me a small favor."

"Anything for the guy who keeps my world free of snow," she replied.

"I have an impromptu parent meeting with one of the kids on the basketball team who's been having trouble keeping his grades up. I was hoping maybe you could watch Brinn for me until I get home. It shouldn't take too long. If you have appointments, I understand, but I just thought I'd try here first." Julia gave his shoulder a friendly tap.

"It's no trouble at all. If you can pick her up and bring her by here, I'll take her home with me when I'm done for the day. We have to make a short stop by the animal hospital but then we'll head home." Julia gave Sam a quick rundown of the morning's events.

"Sounds like you had a busy morning! Hope the poor guy's ok. Brinn will probably want to bring him home. She loves animals!"

"Not a chance," Julia said emphatically. "I'm hoping someone has turned up by now to claim him." The chime of the front entry bell announced that her real appointment had arrived. "Thanks again," Sam said as he left. See you later with Brinn." Julia greeted the young couple she had been expecting. Their meeting was short, with only a few papers to sign. They chatted for a bit and Julia congratulated them on becoming first time home buyers. They left in a state of pure bliss, looking forward to their move and a beautiful future. For the remainder of the afternoon, Julia tended to little tasks that were long overdue. She updated the office listings, transferred some new images to the web site and made copies of information sheets for the open houses that were scheduled for the following weekend. Before she knew it, it was four o'clock. Sam would be coming in any second with Brinn, so Julia wanted to have everything finished up. She closed down her computer, tidied her desk, and switched the office phone over to the answering service. The tinkling of chimes announced the arrival of her young friend, and she smiled in greeting. "Hi there, cutie pie," Julia said to the girl. "Want to come with me to see a new special friend?" Brinn looked up at Julia and nodded. Although Brinn had never spoken to her, Julia chatted away to her as if they were having a normal conversation. "I'll bet you're going to like him!" Brinn silently reached out and took Julia's hand. Julia looked over her head at Sam and smiled. "Better get to your meeting, coach. Brinn and I have places to go and people to see. We'll see you at the house later." Sam smiled and bent down to give Brinn a kiss.

"See you later, pipsqueak. Be good for Julia ok?" Brinn raised her chubby arms to give him a hug, then reached out for Julia's hand once again. Julia wished so much that she would just say something. She recalled how emotional Sam had been when he described what a chatterbox she used to be.

"I would give the world, " he had said, "to hear that magical sound again." The better she got to know them, the more Julia wished for that same thing, for both their sakes.

Chapter 5

Julia continued to chat away to Brinn as she buckled her into her booster seat. "Your Daddy told me that you like dogs. And guess what! We're going to go see one right now." As they headed across town to the veterinary clinic Brinn sat silently watching the world go by. It was so baffling how a little girl could be so alert and interested in everything that was going on around her, but never use her voice. The professionals agreed that the best thing anyone could do was just give it time. And most importantly, they encouraged everyone to keep talking to her. They felt that eventually she would just pick up where she left off, and that there should be no impact on her future speech development. It was fortunate, they said, that she was quite advanced in her language and communication skills before the accident, so the impact of the trauma should be minimal. Julia's heart went out to both of them and as a friend and neighbor she tried to help as much as she could. "Here we are, sweetie" Julia called over her shoulder as they pulled into the parking lot. "Let's go see my new friend." She unbuckled Brinn and took her hand to walk inside. Brenda looked up from her computer as they entered. She came around the end of the counter and showed them into an examining room.

"I'll tell Dr. Westwood you're here. He'll be right in." Brinn climbed into one of the brown vinyl chairs and took everything in as only kids can.

"She must have a million questions," Julia thought. Brent came into the room a few minutes later. He smiled at Julia and gave the tassel on Brinn's hat a little tug.

"How are you today, Brinn. Come to meet Julia's new friend, have you?" Julia laughed. She didn't even know this dog and suddenly it was her friend!

"How is he doing?" she asked.

"See for yourself," Brent replied. He opened the back door of the room and in limped a much cleaner, much happier dog than she had left there that morning. One leg was wrapped completely in white medical tape, but he got around surprisingly well on his three good legs. His tail created quite a windstorm in the small space. He ran immediately up to Brinn and gave her face a big wet lick. Brinn blinked in surprise and then encircled the dog's entire scruff with her two arms, burying her face in the soft fur. Julia let the two of them get acquainted while she and Brent discussed the dog's condition. Brent told her the leg was merely sprained, and that it should be fine in a few weeks. He also said he had called around to the local shelter and to other veterinarians in the area to see if anyone had reported a dog missing or lost. Unfortunately, no one had reported such a dog, and no one seemed familiar with him from the description Brent had given them.

"Well what happens now?" Julia asked. Dog lover or not, she felt bad for the poor guy. He was probably missing his people and his home. Brent gave a slight shrug and told her there were basically two options that they could consider. The first would be to take him straight away to the local shelter where he would be cared for until his owners showed up. If no one came to claim him, then they would do their best to adopt him out to a good home. He would be safe, and cared for in the shelter, but, he added, it can be a very scary situation for some dogs. The second option, would be for someone to take him home and care for him while trying to locate the owners. That way, he would be in a home environment, and be much less traumatized. Then the good doctor also said that it would be impossible for him to take the dog since he and his family were about to leave for their annual ski vacation. His patients were all being cared for by the veterinarian over in Wilmot while he was going to be away. He raised his eyebrows and smiled. "Want to take a dog home, Julia?"

"Me?" Julia said, flabbergasted. "I haven't had a dog since I was a kid, and I only had that one for a little while. I wouldn't know what to do with him!"

"There isn't really much to it," Brent assured her. "He needs food, water and exercise. A few scratches behind the ears, and a belly rub or two, and you're good! Just lookie there," he said pointing to Brinn who was still wrapped around the dog. "I think she can show you how it's done!" Julia stood there stunned, for few minutes letting the idea of bringing a strange, rather large, extremely furry four footed creature into her house, sink in. It would be a challenge, that's for sure. But she had to admit those big brown eyes were winning her over, and she knew she would feel guilty about putting him in a shelter. She realized suddenly, that Brent was still talking to her. "No pressure," he was saying. "But I really do need to close the office and get home to pack. The wife and kids will be chomping at the bit to get on the road."

"Oh, sorry, sorry," Julia stammered. "Ok. I'll take him with me. Wish me luck!" Brent snapped a leash onto the collar and walked the dog out to the car for her while she got Brinn settled in. He also gave her a bag of dry food, a couple of feeding bowls and a box of treats from his supply in the office.

"This ought to do you for a while," he said. "Maybe you'll be lucky and someone will call about him soon. "Good luck."

"Thanks, I think I'm going to need it!" Julia replied. The dog was settled in the back seat on the blanket that was still there from the morning. Julia thought how that already seemed like ages ago. "All set?" she said to Brinn as she started the car. In the rearview mirror all she could see was the beaming face of a three year old who was completely infatuated with her riding companion. "I guess we need to think of a name to call this guy," Julia said to herself as much as her small passenger. "I think we should call him Lucky, since it was lucky for him that he wasn't badly hurt this morning. Yep, Lucky it is. At least until we find out your real name!" The rest of the ride home was oddly quiet. Julia couldn't help but believe that having a preschooler and a dog together in a car should make for some degree of noise if not total chaos. What she had instead was silence, with a child who wouldn't speak and a dog that had suddenly become, for lack of a better word, homesick.

He was sprawled across the back seat with his head resting on his paws and his eyes closed. Brinn had one hand resting on his head but she was back to watching the cars whiz by her window. Julia used the quiet time to form an action plan for finding the owner. Thank goodness it was the weekend. With any luck at all, "Lucky" would be home with his people very soon.

The rest of the afternoon was taken up with settling "Lucky" into his new, temporary home. Julia placed the food bowls in a corner of the mud room and filled one of them with water. The dog lapped up most of the first dish with a lot of enthusiasm and very little grace. In seconds the floor was covered with water and drool, a combination that Julia soon learned was almost lethal on laminate flooring. After nearly slipping flat on her backside, she placed a large rubber backed rug from the laundry room under the two bowls. This seemed to help catch most of the mess. "Oh boy," Julia muttered under her breath. "Do I have some learning to do!" Brinn busied herself following along behind the dog as he went from room to room checking out his new environment. Satisfied that it met his approval, he finally settled down in the centre of the living room carpet. Brinn stretched out beside him and seemed content just to lie there and stoke his fur. It seemed to have a very soothing effect on her, and though she said nothing, there seemed to be a real connection between the two of them. Julia made the most of the quiet time and started on her plan. First she took a digital photo of Lucky and scanned it into her computer. Then she set to work designing a "Found Dog" flyer. She planned to pin them up all over town and in the local shops. She hoped that someone would recognize his picture. The next course of action would be phone calls to all the local animal hospitals and veterinarians, as well as the local shelter and the police station. She didn't know how people would actually go about finding a lost dog, but those seemed like the most obvious places to start. She finished up the poster and connected to the internet to create a list of places to call. By the time she had a pretty good list of numbers, the dog was up pacing around with Brinn trailing right behind. Suddenly he stopped pacing and stood in front of the door casting sideways glances over in Julia's direction. When she made no move to get up, he walked over to her, nudged her hand and walked back and stood in front of the door again. He was on his way back for a second nudge before she clued in. "Ok, I get it. You'll have to cut me some slack here, my friend. I don't know much about dogs you know!" She coaxed him over to the side door that led to a fenced back yard and let him out. Brinn watched from the window as he ploughed through the untouched snow from yesterday's storm. Before long the pristine yard looked like a maze designed by some mad scientist. There were numerous trails heading off in all directions, each one it seemed, marked with brownish yellow spots every few feet. Then to top it all off, there was a nice big brown mound right next to the walkway. Julia sighed. "It's only temporary," she kept reminding herself. Making a mental note to shovel that up after Brinn went home, she shut down her computer and all three of them settled down in the living room to watch some cartoons, Julia on the loveseat and Brinn and the dog on the floor. That's where they were when Sam arrived about an hour later. He gave Brinn a big hug and gave the dog a friendly scratch behind the ears. He seemed every bit as comfortable with the dog as Brinn. After Julia explained why the dog was there, his only comment was something about how lucky the dog was to have been in an accident with such a special person. Julia wasn't sure how lucky she felt, but she did feel flattered by the compliment. It took some convincing to get Brinn away from the dog and into her coat. They only had to walk around to the other side of the house, but it was too cold out to go even that short distance without her gear. The dog seemed equally distressed at her leaving and they shared a long hug before Sam finally pulled her away. Once she was gone, Lucky curled up once again on the rug, looking very pitiful and rejected. Julia wondered if maybe he was part of a family with children. Or maybe, she thought, he just sensed that Brinn needed a friend that also lived in a world without words.

Chapter 6

Julia busied herself preparing a simple supper of soup and a sandwich. The big brown mutt made himself comfortable at her feet, right in the middle of the floor. Every step she took from fridge to counter to stove, involved stepping over his furry mass. Oddly enough, this really didn't bother her. In fact, she was amazed at how quickly she was adapting to his presence, and how pleasant it was to have another "someone" in the house. It also made her remember just why it was that she had never had a dog growing up, or at least why she had never had another dog.

There had been a dog in their house once. She was about 9 and her little brother was 7. They were an inseparable pair, she and Jimmy. Many a long summer day was spent hunting for frogs at the pond, swimming at the beach or playing board games in their tree house hideaway. And always by their side was a small mixed breed dog named Scruffy. Being what they thought was a mix of spaniel and terrier, he had hair that went in all directions. Their Mom had said he looked scruffy the day they brought him home from their grandparents farm, and the name had stuck. Scruffy he was. Everywhere Julia and Jimmy went, Scruffy went too. When he couldn't be with them, he would sleep in the yard or in the mud room anxiously awaiting their return. Every day he would be at the end of the drive waiting for the school bus. There was never a lot of traffic on the country road where they lived. Most of the time the road was only travelled by the people who lived there and who were aware that small children and dogs lived in the area. But one day everything changed, and that day was the last memory she had of having a dog. When Julia and Jimmy got off the bus, Scruffy was nowhere to be seen. As the bus driver pulled away, Julia and Jimmy saw Scruffy running towards them from across the road. In his delight to see Scruffy, Jimmy ran into the road just as Scruffy crossed into the intersection. They were both struck by an oncoming car. For months afterwards, Julia relived those horrifying moments every time she closed her eyes. She saw

Scruffy flying through the air and landing in the ditch. And she saw Jimmy lying there, so still in front of the car. Jimmy suffered a broken leg and some pretty serious scrapes and bruises but otherwise he was fine. Scruffy, being so small, had not survived the impact. By the time some other motorists who had stopped to help checked on him in the ditch he was already gone. With Jimmy in a cast and unable to play much, he and Julia spent long hours together in the tree house mourning the loss of their dear companion. Their parents, terrified by how close they had come to losing a child, unjustly laid the blame for the whole thing on Scruffy. When Julia and Jimmy had one day requested that they get another dog, they were met with outright refusal. And so the years had passed with requests made and requests denied until eventually they stopped asking. There would be no more dogs for their family. Julia hadn't thought about those days for a very long time. And now, here she was with a dog in her house once again. She made a mental note to call Jimmy on the weekend and tell him about her new houseguest. As she enjoyed her supper, Lucky snored at her feet in front of the fire. After a while she decided she had better let him out again before they settled in for the night. "Come on Lucky," she said as she walked to the door. When he didn't respond, she repeated, "Lucky, let's go." Walking over to him, to get his attention, she realized he probably wasn't coming because Lucky wasn't really his name. "No worries, " she said as she gave his head a scratch. "We'll find out your real name soon enough." Once the final evening rituals were accomplished, both lady and dog settled down for the night. Julia thought that Lucky would probably sleep by the fireplace in the living room where she had placed a blanket for him earlier. But she thought wrong. Apparently this guy was used to sharing someone's bed. While she was in the bathroom getting into her pajamas, he made himself quite comfortable in the middle of her bed. "Well now," she said, making "get off" motions with her arms. "This just isn't going to happen. Get your furry feet down here on the floor and park yourself somewhere." She walked with him out to the living room and pointed to his blanket. "How about you sleep here?" she tried to say forcefully. She walked back to her room and crawled under the covers. Not two seconds later she heard the distinct clickety clack of nails coming across the hardwood. Sure enough when she raised her head from the pillow there were two brown eyes staring back at her. Deciding he was lonely in his new surroundings, Julia went and retrieved his blanket from the other room. She spread it out on top of the area rug beside her bed. "There you go. Close but not too close." Lucky seemed happy enough with this offering. After scrunching the blanket into a suitable heap, and circling about three or four times, he plunked himself down with a big sigh. For the rest of the night they both slept soundly, both dreaming about finding Lucky's real home.

Chapter 7

It was hours later before a passing motorist came upon the old truck and its injured river. By that time the temperature had plummeted and a good bit of snow had fallen through the open doors of the truck. The passerby called 911 and threw a blanket over the old man who remained slumped over the twisted metal of the steering wheel. Dried blood had crusted over his eye and his legs were entwined with the crumpled metal of the front end. In a matter of minutes the paramedics arrived and had him in an ambulance heading for the Wilmot hospital. His vital signs were extremely weak and they hoped he would make it that far. They had checked the truck and the surrounding area for any other passengers but stated in their report that he had been the lone occupant of the vehicle. Once he was safely transferred into the capable hands of the hospital staff, they returned to their post to await the calls that they knew would come as a result of today's storm.

Henry survived the ambulance trip and was stabilized in the emergency room. He had not regained consciousness and his condition was marked as critical. Doctors were most concerned that the combination of hypothermia, blood loss and shock might be more than the old man's system could handle. The next few hours would be very crucial and he would be under extremely close observation. His wallet had provide a name and number of next of kin. A daughter who unfortunately lived across the country was contacted and she had assured the staff that she would be there as soon as she possibly could. In the meantime, she requested that someone be sent to the old man's home to care for his dog until she arrived. The hospital had notified the local shelter, and they had promised to send both an agent from the ASPCA and a police officer to the home as soon as possible. When they arrived, there was no dog anywhere to be found.

Chapter 8

Julia was enjoying her first cup of morning coffee when she heard a small tap on her side door. Wondering who might be coming to call so early, she tightened the sash on her robe and headed for the door. She was nearly bowled over by seventy pounds of dog that wanted to get there first. Lucky's tail was wagging like the blades of a helicopter and creating just about as much wind. Julia had to push her way in front of him to get the door open. When she did, Lucky bounded out nearly knocking their early morning guest off her feet. Her father was standing off to the side. "Morning Julia. Sorry to stop by so early but we were on our way out and Brinn dragged me over to your door. Guess she wanted to say hi to this guy!" Brinn had both arms wrapped around Lucky who was licking her face for all he was worth. The entire picture was one of pure bliss.

"No problem," Julia assured him. "I needed to get a move on anyway. I'm planning to put some posters up around town to see if we can find this guy's rightful owner. I think he's missing his home." Sam glanced down at the dog and his daughter.

"I don't know. He sure seems to be happy enough here!" Julia nodded. "He does really come to life when he sees Brinn. Maybe he's staying at the wrong house!" Sam chuckled. "I hadn't really ever thought about getting Brinn a dog. Maybe a dog would help to bring back her spirit."

Julia agreed. "Maybe you should give that some thought." They exchanged pleasantries for a few more minutes and then Sam told Brinn it was time to go. They were heading into Wilmot to pick up some workbooks for the team that Sam had dropped off at the printers.

"You're heading into Wilmot?" Julia asked. "Do you think you could do me a favor?"

"Sure, anything," Sam replied. Julia walked over to her computer desk and came back with some papers in her hand.

"Could you hand out a few of these to the shop owners in town? I'm going to do Lilac Creek and the rural areas, but I think it might be a good idea for the folks in Wilmot to know about Lucky too. You just never know!." Sam took the papers from her.

"No problem. I'll stop at as many places as I can." He told Brinn to give Lucky one last hug so they could be going. It took all of Julia's strength to keep Lucky from following them down the drive.

"Not so fast there, big fella. We've got places to go and people to see too." Lucky hung his head and returned to his previous spot under the kitchen table. Julia finished the last of her coffee, took her cup to the sink and headed off to get dressed. Lucky watched her every move but made no effort to get up. "Good," she muttered. "You stay right there. I'll be a lot faster if I'm not tripping over you." As if he understood, or maybe because he was sulking over not being allowed to go with his new little friend, Lucky stayed put. Dressed in a sweater and jeans, Julia emerged from the bedroom carrying more paperwork, a box of thumbtacks, tape, small nails and a hammer. She was going to be prepared to slap up a poster wherever possible. She compiled all her supplies into a small plastic box with a lid and handle. She kept out the sheet of paper containing all the addresses of local veterinary offices, animal clinics, and the local shelter. Then she made a second list that put all the places she wanted to visit into the most logical order for driving. She had considered a simple phone call to each of them, but she felt going in person with Lucky at her side would make a more memorable impression. She hoped that by seeing Lucky, someone might recognize him, or be aware of any missing or lost dog reports. It was going to be a long day, for sure, but hopefully one that would return some positive results. Snapping a leash onto Lucky's collar they headed to the car. Julia was glad that the snow had stopped falling. The roads would be cleared and that would make the day a lot easier. She got Lucky into the back seat, put all of her supplies on the front passenger seat and got herself settled behind the wheel. "Ok my furry friend. Off we go to see if anybody recognizes you!" Responding to the excited tone of her voice, Lucky gave a big woof from the back seat. Julia laughed at his enthusiasm and pondered for a moment how much fun it was to chat with "someone" who agreed with everything you said. She hated to admit it, but she was also getting a little too attached to this mutt already. Maybe she would consider a dog of her own once Lucky's situation was resolved. Ten minutes later they had arrived at their first stop, the local animal shelter. Lucky could hear all the other dogs barking and thought maybe it was playtime. He jumped down from the back seat and took off nearly dislocating Julia's arm. Julia reeled him back under control as they went through the front door. The young girl behind the desk was wearing bright colored scrubs printed with cartoon cats and dogs. Her smile was equally cheery and she greeted both Julia and Lucky with genuine enthusiasm. "Good morning," she chirped. "My name is Gwen. What can I do for you two?" Julia extended her hand,

"I'm Julia and this is Lucky. Well his name's not really Lucky, but that's what I've been calling him."

"Ok," said the receptionist looking rather quizzical. "How can I help you and Lucky?" Gwen listened as Julia recited the whole story, and thought for a moment before making any comment. "We haven't had anyone in looking for a lost dog as far as I know," she said. "But let me just check the log book from last night to make sure." After a few minutes she looked up from the notebook. "Nope, sorry. Were you hoping to leave the dog here until the owner is located?

"Oh, no," Julia said quickly. "I've got him sort of settled in at my place. I'd hate for him to have to adjust to another new place. Besides, we're becoming pretty good friends, and he absolutely adores the little girl next door!" Gwen smiled as she scratched the dog's floppy ears.

"Looks like you really are Lucky! But I'm sure you'd like to find your real owner, wouldn't you?" Once again Lucky showed off his uncanny understanding of the English language by woofing in agreement. Gwen took one of the posters from Julia and promised to let her know right away if anyone called or came looking for a dog that resembled Lucky. Julia thanked her warmly and headed back to the car. She was a little disappointed that nothing had come of that visit. She thought the shelter would be the first place someone would look for a lost dog. "Someone has to be looking for you," she said as she got Lucky settled into the car again." For the rest of the day they got in and out of the car, talking to shop keepers, nailing posters on light posts, and visiting other local establishments in hopes that someone would recognize Lucky. By the time they got back home she was tired and disappointed. Lucky seemed to sense her mood, and nosed her hand as she sat on the porch with a cold drink.

They hadn't been home more than five minutes when Brinn came running down the veranda from her house. She collapsed on the porch beside Lucky and they resumed their hugging where they had left off that morning. Behind her, Sam shrugged apologetically. "I just can't keep her away," he said. "there's just some sort of connection there that's hard to ignore."

"Don't worry about it, "Julia assured him. "I think it's terrific." "I haven't seen Brinn look this happy since I've known you two!" Sam nodded.

"Makes me almost wish we could keep him. But there has to be someone out there whose missing him and wants him back." Julia nodded in agreement. "I just wish we could find them." Sam assured her that he had spoken to everyone he could think of over in Wilmot. "Lucky's happy mug is nailed to every post and bulletin board I could find, but no one seemed to know of any runaway dogs. Any idea what you'll do if nobody claims him?" Julia shook her head and shrugged. "I really don't know. I hate the thought of taking him to the shelter. What if nobody wants to adopt him. He is pretty big, and I don't think he's all that young. He does seem to really like kids, though," she gestured toward Brinn and Lucky who had become one single mass of brown fur and fuzzy red coat.

"Maybe you should consider adopting him," she teased. Sam looked at her surprised, as though the thought hadn't occurred to him before. His voice was hesitant when he said, "Ya, maybe I should. Might be just what Brinn needs!" Julia laughed. "You actually sound serious," she said. "I think that would be awesome, but, maybe we're getting a little ahead of ourselves. I still think Lucky would be happiest back with his real people. A dog his age is probably really attached to somebody."

"You're right," Sam agreed. "Maybe I'll give the idea of a dog some thought, though." After giving Brinn a few more minutes with Lucky, they headed back home to finish their day. Julia watched the sky turn the dark purple of evening, her thoughts on the events of the day. When she made a move to get up, Lucky was right beside her. She smiled and gave his head a pat. "Let's call it a day, old boy. Maybe tomorrow....."

Chapter 9

Wendy arrived at the hospital nearly two days after her father was admitted. She was directed to the critical care unit by a very friendly nurse whose name tag read Sherry. "If you just identify yourself at the nurse's station there, they'll page Dr. Connor for you." Wendy thanked her and headed for the elevator. She was tired, hungry, and most of all worried. She had really hoped to find her father awake and on the mend. Learning that he was still in the critical care unit could only mean bad news. She exited the elevator on the third floor and found the nurse's station, introducing herself right away. The nurse punched some numbers into the phone on her desk while Wendy paced the hallway. In a few minutes, the nurse found her and explained that Dr. Connor was just finishing up in surgery and would meet with her in about half an hour. "Would you like to sit with your father while you wait?"

"Absolutely," Wendy replied, and followed the nurse down the hall. She was not at all prepared for what she saw. Her father looked so frail and small in the huge bed. His face was a sickening shade of gray and there were tubes and wires connected to him everywhere. In the background she could hear the steady humming and beeping of the medical machinery that she knew must be keeping him alive. "Oh, Dad," was all she could say. Wendy pulled a chair up close to the bed and tried to hold her father's hand without disturbing the needle that seemed to be weighing his hand down. She prayed that he would open his eyes and speak to her, or maybe even squeeze her hand to let her know that he knew she was there. She wanted so badly to let him know that he was not alone. But he remained silent and unmoving. She sat there with him, thinking about the many times since her mother's death that she had begged him to move closer to her. He just kept saying he wasn't ready to do that yet. Well maybe this would change the situation. Maybe the doctors could help her convince him that he should be near someone who could help take care of him. Maybe now he would agree that it was finally time. Wendy was lost in these thoughts when Dr. Connor quietly entered the room. The look of compassion in his eyes as he introduced himself, made Wendy's heart sink. She could tell bad news was coming. "I'm Dr. Connor," he said offering his hand. "I've been looking after your father since he was brought in." Wendy shook his hand and introduced herself, asking the question she wasn't sure she really wanted answered. "How is he, Dr.?" Dr. Connor took a deep breath and motioned for her to be seated. He pulled up a second chair and faced her. "Your father was suffering from shock and hypothermia when he was admitted. He had lost some blood, but that wasn't as serious as the first two issues. The paramedics were able to stabilize him enroute to the hospital, and we were hopeful at first that his condition would continue to improve. Unfortunately, before he was able to make much headway, he suffered a major stroke and hasn't regained consciousness since. We're still hopeful that he may come around so we can better access the damage that he's suffered. Right now it's just a waiting game. I'm so sorry." Wendy sat speechless and let this news sink in. She could feel the tears welling up, and she didn't want to lose control. She was able to speak enough to thank the doctor and ask if it was alright for her to remain at his bedside. "Of course," he replied. "The nurses are just down the hall if you need anything or if you have any questions. If you decide to go home and get some rest, just leave a number with them and they'll call you immediately if there is any change." He shook Wendy's hand once again and left the room. Wendy settled back into her spot beside the bed. Sooner or later she would go back to the hotel for some rest. And then she would have to find out who was looking after Jasper. But for now she just wanted to sit here and hold the hand of the man she had loved and looked up to her entire life.

Chapter 10

Julia sighed as she got ready for work Monday morning. Nothing
had happened over the weekend to get them any closer to finding
Lucky's owner. Now she was faced with the question of what to do
with a dog while she went to work. She hadn't considered this
because she had really expected Lucky to be out of her life by now.
She ran through her appointments for the day. Two house
showings, one meeting at the office with clients, and her obligatory
two hours of office duty. She was meeting her clients at the homes
she was showing, so Lucky could come with her and wait in her car.
The meeting at the office and her office time would be another
matter altogether. Somehow Lucky just didn't fit the "bring your
dog to work" profile. She could leave him at home, she supposed,
and rush over between her showings and her meeting to let him
out. But the thought of leaving him alone and unoccupied in her
tiny house terrified her. She imagined all kinds of disaster, from
him chewing up all her shoes to him somehow being adept enough
to get into her cupboards and eat everything in sight! At the very
least, she envisioned puddles and piles that would stain the floors
and smell horrific if he wasn't able to hold it all until she got there.

She was jostled from her imaginings of doggy disasters when the
doorbell rang. As usual, Lucky was determined to get there first
and blocked her path to the door completely. "Unless you plan to
open that door, you better move aside and let me pass," she
grumbled, thoughts of all the trouble he had not even caused yet,
making her mood less than positive. When he finally let her get the
door open, it was Brinn who stood on the other side, with Sam
following, as always, some steps behind. He couldn't be more
apologetic. "I'm sorry, I'm sorry," he repeated. She just opens the
door and runs down here. I sure hope you can get this dog sent off
before you decide to evict us," he said with a helplessness that
melted her heart. Julia laughed. "Don't be silly. It's good to see
Brinn so happy. But I am sorry to report that nothing has
happened to move us closer to that event. In fact, I was just trying

to figure out what to do with him while I go to work." Sam broke in. "I thought that might be a problem," "And I think we might have an easy solution."

"Oh Ya?" Julia asked, eyebrows raised. "And what might that be?"

"Well, I'm off this week while the kids write exams. So I was thinking maybe the old guy could hang out with us. During the day, of course, then you could have him back at night. That would work for this week anyway, and maybe by then...." He shrugged and raided his palms in a who knows kind of gesture. Julia couldn't believe her good fortune. Thinking about organizing work and a dog for the week had really started to freak her out, and she hoped she could extend her good luck even further. "Actually," she drew out the word, "what would you think of keeping him entirely at your house for the week. I have evening showings scheduled almost every night and office duty every day. Would that be an insane favor to ask of you?" Sam laughed outright. "I wanted to suggest the same thing but I figured you wouldn't give the mutt up for that long. We'd love to have a furry houseguest for the week."

"Then it's settled. He's all yours until Saturday or until we find out where he belongs." She gathered up all of Lucky's things and put them in a bag. She clipped the leash to his collar and watched as Sam walked away, so happy behind the little girl he loved with all his heart, and the great big dog that had brought back her smile.

Chapter 11

Wendy eventually returned to the hotel to unpack and get some rest. Nothing had changed with her Dad but she left explicit instructions to call her if anything changed. She was only a short ten minute drive from the hospital so she was pretty comfortable leaving for a while. She also wanted to get out to her Dad's place and make sure everything was okay there. Her main concern was for Jasper, her Dad's dog. Wendy knew he was getting pretty old, but her Dad had never said anything about him being ill. She hadn't yet had a chance to ask if anyone had gone out to the house as she had requested. Right now all she wanted to think about was a warm bath, a hot cup of tea and a soft pillow. But it had been almost three days since her dad had been brought to the hospital. What if jasper was alone and hungry in the house. She knew she wouldn't be able to rest until she had at least tried to do something. Wendy sat for a moment to try and clear her head. It was too late now to drive out to the house, and being on the road or out at her Dad's place would put her quite a bit farther from the hospital should anything happen. Wendy knew that many of the old neighbors that had lived nearby while she was growing up had all moved away. New young families had moved into many of the homes, and her Dad wasn't much at socializing, especially not since her Mom had passed away. In their telephone conversations, he talked mostly about Jasper, what kinds of fish were biting, and how many repairs he had to make on the old Chevy. She couldn't actually remember him even mentioning any neighbors or friends of late. And then it hit her. Dr. Montrose, her dad's eye doctor had a daughter who lived two houses down the road. Her Dad had been diagnosed with early signs of glaucoma and he was being monitored very closely. If she were to contact Dr. Montrose, maybe he would have his daughter take a run over to the house. Wendy glanced around the room for a telephone directory but not wanting to waste any more time, pulled out her cell and dialed directory assistance. In a matter of seconds she was connected to Dr. Montrose's office which gave her his emergency number. She quickly jotted the number down and then dialed. When the doctor answered she explained the situation as best she could, and was so relieved to hear his helpful response. He assured her that his daughter would be happy to drop by and check on the farm. Wendy left him her cell number and thanked him for all his help. With that matter taken care of, she finally headed to the little kitchenette to prepare that much needed cup of tea.

Not more than an hour later her cell phone rang. Thinking it was too soon to be hearing back from Dr. Montrose, she automatically assumed it was the hospital calling. Trying to prepare herself for bad news, she took a deep breath and pushed the talk button and said hello. "Wendy?" a female voice questioned. "This is Alison Grant calling, Dr. Montrose is my father." It took Wendy a few minutes to realize that she wasn't speaking from someone at the hospital after all. "Hello, are you still there?" the voice asked again. Wendy finally found her voice. "Yes, I'm sorry. I was expecting this call to be from the hospital."

"That's ok, I understand," the young woman continued. "I just wanted to let you know that I was at your Dad's place just now. Everything is just fine, but Jasper wasn't there. There were food bowls in the kitchen and one of the dishes was filled with water. There was also a bag of dog food beside the fridge. Oh, and Jasper's leash was on a hook by the back door. Do you know if he was with your Dad when the accident happened?" Wendy tried to remember what the police had said when they contacted her. She was pretty sure that they had reported him being alone. But then would they even think to check the area out for a dog? She returned her attention back to the caller. "I don't really know. I guess we'll have to look in to that. But thank you so much for going over there for me. At least I won't have to worry about him being out there alone and hungry. Thank you again." The young woman replied with genuine concern. "It was no trouble at all. If there's anything else I can do please don't hesitate to call. I met your father a few times and he was always so nice. I'm really sorry to hear about his accident." Wendy thanked her again and disconnected. From all indications, it appeared that Jasper was still alive and well. Wendy didn't think the leash hanging by the door meant much. It certainly didn't mean that the dog hadn't accompanied her Dad that day. Henry seldom, if ever used the leash for Jasper. He always said that he kept it hanging there just "in case." Wendy wondered if maybe her Dad had left Jasper with someone else when he had gone out. Or had he left Jasper outside to wait for him? Had the dog decided to go looking for Henry when he hadn't returned? Maybe the dog was sick and at the vets. All of these thoughts ran through Wendy's head as she prepared her bath, and tried to plan out her tasks for the next day. She knew when her father woke up, Jasper would be the first thing on his mind. He was totally devoted to the animal, and losing him would surely set her Dad's recovery back some. "I just have to find him before Dad wakes up and finds out he's missing." This was her final thought as she sank into the warm luxury of bubbles.

Chapter 12

The next couple of days flew by in a flurry of appointments and showings. Julia was up to her eyeballs in paperwork as well. With spring just a couple of months away, it seemed like everyone in town started thinking about buying houses. This was all good of course. On a professional level, life was good. Julia preferred being busy to being bored, and it was nice to have an income that allowed her to be comfortable. On the home front, however, things could be better. There were lots of renovations she still wanted to do, her own apartment could use a little attention in the cleaning department, and she was way behind in her family obligations. She hadn't been out to see her parents in some time, and she had planned to call her brother this weekend but had totally forgotten. The whole new dog in the house situation had really thrown her off her game. Thinking about all of that made her think about Sam. As well as everything else that was sliding, her love life was pathetic as well. It would be nice to have a special someone to share things with. She and Sam were great neighbors and they were becoming really good friends. But could it ever be more than that? He was a really nice guy. He was slim, just a bit taller than herself, with wavy brown hair and blue eyes. Julia was most impressed though, by his easy smile and happy nature, given the hard knocks that life had thrown at him. He was a great teacher and a totally devoted Dad. There wasn't much around the house that he couldn't do, and Julia was so grateful for that. He had saved her from the cash happy hands of contractors more than once over the last year. "Yes, there was a lot to like about Sam Baxter," she mused, the most of which right now was his generosity. If he hadn't taken care of Lucky this week, she didn't know how she would have made it through. Heading home for the day, she thought maybe she would make them all dinner tonight. Sam could fill her in on his dog sitting adventures and she also wanted to ask his opinion of what to do with Lucky should a real owner never show up. She really hoped that things didn't come to that. He was a terrific dog, as dogs go, she assumed. But she didn't feel like now was the time for her to make that choice. On the other hand, she didn't really think she could look into those big brown eyes and hand the leash over to someone at the shelter. "He belongs to somebody!" she muttered out loud. "Why can't we find them!" She made a mental note to call a few more places tomorrow just to keep Lucky fresh in everyone's mind. She also decided to take a drive herself over to Wilmot just to check on the posters that Sam had put up. Wilmot was the next town over from Lilac Creek. It was quite a bit larger, and boasted a small shopping center, several restaurant chains and the closest hospital. There was also an actual police station too, and Julia thought maybe a stop by there might be wise. You never know what folks might report to the police. Maybe somebody had reported a lost dog roaming in the area. It wouldn't be impossible for a dog to run away in Wilmot and end up in Lilac Creek. Maybe someone would recognize him there if they saw him. Yes, she would take Lucky for a road trip to Wilmot the first chance she got. It was already Thursday, and her schedule was light for Friday, so she might be able to head over in the afternoon. She was pretty sure that Sam and Brinn would be more than ready to give Lucky back by then. For now, though, she had better get to the store for some supplies if she was going to cook dinner for guests tonight.

After a quick stop at the local grocery mart she was on her way home. It would be a simple supper of roasted chicken, potatoes and vegetables. She didn't consider herself much of a cook but she could put together simple home cooking without too much stress. Her Dad was a real meat and potatoes kind of guy and that was what their day to day meals had always been. Consequently, Julia was pretty good at pulling together such a meal. Roasted chicken, meat loaf, spaghetti. Stew and pot roast were her specialties. If she had guests for dinner, which wasn't often, they never expected fancy gourmet creations, but they did look forward to some yummy home cooking.

When she pulled into the driveway she could see Brinn and Lucky playing in the yard. Brinn was throwing a stick and Lucky was retrieving it. They both looked deliriously happy. Brinn was smiling from ear to ear and Lucky was drooling like a water fountain gone out of control. But it was so odd to watch them and hear no words. It just boggled the mind that any child could appear to be so happy and yet not speak. Julia sat for a while watching them, expecting any minute to hear Brinn call Lucky's name, or call him to come, or add some terms of endearment to the hugs she was lavishing on him. But there was nothing. It was as though she had completely forgotten how to use language. Her heart ached for the little girl and her Dad. Realizing she had been sitting for a while, and that she needed to get her refrigerated items into the house, Julia gathered everything together and headed in. She was so intent on juggling her bags, purse and office folders that she didn't see Sam heading towards her. He watched with amusement as she kept coming headlong right into him. Her surprise at the impact nearly sent everything flying, but Sam managed to keep her upright and her parcels all intact. "Whoa, there," he laughed. "Not a good idea to rush around with your head down!" Julia caught her breath and smiled back. "Thanks for catching everything. That would have been quite a mess, considering there are eggs in one of those bags!" Sam took a couple of the bags that were swinging from one arm, and carried them inside for her. Julia thanked him and then remembered her reason for buying all the food in the first place. "I was hoping if you weren't busy, that you and Brinn could come for dinner." Sam eyed the chicken, vegetables and fresh baked bread. "Just looking at the groceries you're unpacking is making me drool as bad as that foolish dog out there. We accept your invitation wholeheartedly. I may need to drag Brinn away from that animal to get her washed up."

"No hurry," Julia said. "I'll get things started and you come on in when you're ready." Sam turned towards the back yard, adding over his shoulder that he would bring a bottle of wine. Julia smiled. It was going to be a fun evening.

Not more than a half hour later, there was a tap at her door. Sam entered first carrying a bottle of wine, followed by Lucky dragging a beaming Brinn close behind. "Hi guys." Julia greeted them warmly, taking the wine form Sam, giving Brinn a hug and Lucky a scratch behind the ears all at the same time. Brinn unsnapped

Lucky's leash and they headed immediately for the living room rug in front of the fireplace. Sam followed Julia into the kitchen with an offer to help with dinner. They chatted amiably about the week's events, and Sam suddenly became quiet and pensive. "What's on your mind?" Julia queried. "Did things not go well with Lucky? Did he do something you're afraid to tell me about?" Sam snapped out of his daze and laughed when he realized what she was asking. "No, quite the opposite, in fact." He met her eyes directly but hesitated before proceeding. Slowly, he spoke. "Actually," he said, "things went very well. So well in fact, that I was going to ask you if you might consider letting us keep Lucky. Until his owners are found, of course." He paused and then went on. "You see, I haven't seen Brinn this happy, this lively, this.....he searched for a word...this connected, in a very long time. I think Lucky has been the reason. Even though she still hasn't spoken, I sense that we're definitely making progress in that direction. I'd love to keep Lucky around for a while to see what happens." Sam looked down at his shoes almost shyly. "I'm actually feeling a bit guilty," he said. "I find myself hoping that Lucky's owners don't turn up and you'll let us keep him." Julia looked at him with genuine surprise. She didn't know quite what to say. After a bit she realized Sam was waiting for some kind of response. "Well, that's very......interesting," she stammered. "I have to admit, I'm surprised. I just naturally figured that you would be finding the idea of suddenly being a dog owner as weird as I had. Guess I was wrong!" For a moment neither of them spoke. Sam finally broke the silence. "Well, what do you think?" Julia paused only for a second before responding with, "I think it's wonderful!" She gave Sam a big hug. She admitted to him that she had been getting a little worried about what she would do if his owners didn't turn up. She confessed that, as much as it had been a new adventure, dog ownership was just not something she wanted to undertake right now. "I think I'll want a dog someday," she said. "But I want to be at a different place in my life than I am right now. I'm not sure I could give a dog enough attention with the way things are. But I think it's an awesome idea for you and Brinn, especially Brinn." Sam was grinning from ear to ear. "It's settled then. Lucky stays with us." Then Julia spoke solemnly. "But have you thought about how it might affect Brinn to have to give him up, after she's become so attached?" Sam nodded. "I considered that a lot, before I brought the whole idea up. I think I've explained it it terms she can understand. I told her we were just taking care of Lucky for a while, and that he wasn't ours to keep, or as she used to say "for keeps." But, honestly I think even when Lucky's owner is found, we'll have made enough progress that it will be worth it. If Brinn starts to speak, then we'll be able to discuss getting our own dog. At least I'm really hoping that's how it all turns out!" Julia's serious expression transformed into a grin. "I know that's how it will be! We just have to let Lucky work his magic! Now how about a glass of that wine while the chicken cooks!"

Chapter 13

Wendy awoke to the sound of her cell phone. Her pulse quickened as she fumbled to find the device on her bedside table. "Hello," she said expectantly.

"Could I speak with Mrs. Coldwell, please?" asked a soft female voice.

"Speaking." Wendy replied.

"This is Sherry calling from Wilmot Hospital. I have some good news about your father." Wendy felt her muscles relax and her grip on the phone lighten. "Good news?" she repeated. The bit of hesitation on the other end did not go unnoticed. Then Sherry continued. "Yes, it is good news. Your father is awake, now and is trying to speak to us. He's a little incoherent, but he's been asking for you and mumbling about someone that sounds like Jasper. He's still very critical of course, but his being awake is a good sign. We wanted to let you know right away." Wendy thanked her and said she would be there as soon as she could. Wendy was so relieved that it hadn't been bad news that she just flopped back into bed to let her nerves relax. Once she had gained her composure, she showered and dressed with thoughts of what to tell her Dad about Jasper running through her head. She really didn't have any news, or even any leads for that matter. It was going to be so hard to tell him that Jasper was lost. But then, on the other hand, maybe her Dad knew where Jasper was, and could let her know. Guess she would have to get over there and talk to him so she could clear up some of the confusion.

The short trip to the hospital didn't give her a lot of time to think about how she would break the news about Jasper to her dad. She was really far more concerned about her dad's health. She had sensed some hesitation on the part of the nurse, and she figured there was more news to come. But for now, she was happy that he was awake and that she would be able to speak to him. She really wanted him to know that she was there, that he wasn't alone. She knew that strokes could have varying degrees of severity. She couldn't help hoping that the fact that he could speak was a good sign. Wendy parked the car as close to the hospital as she could and hurried inside. Dr. Connor was in the room with her dad when she entered. He was writing notes on her dad's chart and speaking to the nurses at the same time, no doubt giving some directions as to his further care. Wendy waited for a moment before walking up to her dad's bed. The doctor and nurse stepped aside so she could greet her dad. She took his hand and told him that she was there. He responded immediately to her voice and squeezed her hand. "Wendy," he said in a raspy whisper. "You're here." Tears sprang to Wendy's eyes, and she had to fight to maintain control. "Hi Dad. I'm here" In the next gravely breath he spoke with more animation. "Jasper. Where's Jasper?" Wendy tried to calm him. "It's ok, Dad. Right now you need to stay calm and still."

"Can't......Jasper...hurt....lost....cold...hungry," with each of the single drawn out words, her Dad became more and more anxious. Wendy squeezed his hand. "We're trying to find him Dad, but we didn't know if he was with you in the truck. He must have run off for help. We'll find him, Dad. But you need to relax so you're well when we find him." Her Dad's grip on her hand relaxed. His eyes were growing heavy and he seemed to be dropping off, then he spoke again. "Find Jasper," he rattled and then was asleep. Wendy let go of his hand and rose to speak to the doctor. He read the question in her eyes, and suggested they go down the hall to the lounge to talk. Wendy tried to prepare herself for the worst. Once they were seated, she immediately asked, "How is he really?" Dr. Connor shrugged slightly and his lips formed a thin line. "It really doesn't look good. Early tests indicate that your father suffered a fair amount of brain damage to the areas that control physical movement and body functions. He is basically paralyzed from the waist down. He seems to have some arm movements and his speech is pretty good. His memory appears to be good as well, although some confusion is to be expected. It's early yet to determine what his true abilities will be. I feel pretty confident in saying that he will require constant care. A long term care facility would probably be best." Wendy sat quietly for a while letting all the information sink in. It really wasn't the news she had been praying for. She realized the doctor was speaking again. "For now, we have to concentrate on getting him past the injuries from the accident and het his vitals stabilized. Once he's stronger, we can conduct some further tests to see how best to proceed. Do you have any questions?" Wendy shook her head. There were probably a thousand things she needed to ask, but she couldn't think of them right now. She thanked the doctor and headed back to her Dad's room. "Oh, Dad," she thought as she sat beside him again. "What are we going to do now?" The early morning hours passed as she sat there thinking and waiting. Eventually he stirred slightly and reached out for her hand. His eyes were still closed when his lips again formed the word...."Jasper." Wendy sat bolt upright with a definite sense of purpose. She knew what she had to do first. If her dad was going to get better at all, she was going to have to find Jasper. That's all there was to it. But how? How did one go about finding a lost dog? She didn't=t have the foggiest idea, but she knew she had to try. "Well, no time like the present," she thought. "Might as well get started." She kissed her dad's forehead lightly, pulled the blanket over him, and left the room with a solemn promise to be back with some information about Jasper if it was the last thing she did.

It was late enough in the morning now for stores and businesses to be open. She would start there. In fact, Wendy thought that she remembered that the police station was right across the street. Maybe she would start there.

Chapter 14

Once dinner was over, they all relaxed for a while in front of the fire. Brinn and Lucky sprawled across the rug and Sam and Julia sat side by side on the loveseat. They talked about simple things, their jobs, the weather, and the funny antics of their mutual new found furry friend. Julia had told Sam about her plans to head into Wilmot again to refresh everyone's memory since Sam put the posters up. "I thought maybe, if you didn't mind giving him up for a day, that I would take Lucky with me. Maybe if people see him it will spur some recognition." Sam agreed without hesitation. "Brinn and I have to go to a few appointments, so that should work out fine. And I think you're right. This guy makes a better impression in person than he does in a picture!"

"Settled, then, " said Julia, to which Sam nodded. When Brinn's eyes started to droop and Lucky fell into a twitching doggy dream of rabbit chasing, they decided to call it a day. Sam roused his pair of sleepyheads from the floor and scooped Brinn into his arms for the short trip to their door. Julia covered her with a warm blanket so she didn't need to struggle into a winter coat. Julia opened the door for them and Lucky led the way down the veranda. They said a whispered good night with Sam thanking her yet again for letting Lucky stay with them, and for the delicious dinner. She in turn, thanked him for his help with Lucky and wished him luck. With a simultaneous "See you tomorrow," she closed the door behind them. Julia was torn. She wanted so badly to see Brinn get better. She could see for herself how much happier the little girl was since Lucky came into her life. But she also felt that someone, somewhere, was equally unhappy over losing a beloved pet, and needed to know that he was ok. Well she wouldn't give up the search just yet. She would take a trip to Wilmot as planned, and see if that produced any leads. Then she would call around once again to the places where she had left posters and flyers. If none of that proved fruitful, she would be able to consider leaving Lucky with Sam, her conscience clear. She would know that she had tried her best. And, if she was ultimately able to find Lucky's real owner, she felt confident that Sam and Brinn would continue to move forward with the help of another new furry friend. All in all, it was looking like a win-win situation. Julia went to bed with a light heart and optimistic plans for the next few days.

The sun came up with that brightness that only a frigid winter day can produce. By all appearances, it should be nice and warm outside, when in fact, it was probably one of the coldest days of the year. But cold was ok. Cold and sunny would mean good roads for her trip to Wilmot. After last week's storm, she wasn't in any hurry to drive in snow again. It would happen, of course, because winters here were long and snowy. But for today, Julia planned to dress for the cold and enjoy the sunshine. Her plan was to visit the police station first, and then some of the local clinics and shops where Sam had previously left plenty of lost dog posters. Checking to make sure she had all her necessary winter attire for walking around town, she was finally ready to go. She needed only to stop by Sam's, pick up Lucky and be on her way. At the last minute she remembered the box of dog treats she had purchased for Lucky and grabbed a few for the trip. She was surprised really at how much she was looking forward to the trip. Lucky was good company, the kind who didn't require her to wear her always pleasant, always positive, real estate smile, and the kind you could talk to without having anybody talking back. Yep, it was going to be a good day. Julia decided to double check the street map she had downloaded from Google maps. The location of the police station was identified with a numbered red bubble, as were other establishments that she had entered into the query. It appeared the police station was right across the street from the hospital. Julia figured there was no need to go there, but it would be a helpful landmark. Wilmot wasn't really that big, and Julia was pretty familiar with the subdivisions, from houses that were for sale. But she figured having a map was just added assurance, and could likely save some time. Finally, she was ready. "Look out Wilmot, here we come!" she thought to herself. She closed and locked her door and headed down the verandah to pick up Lucky. Brinn opened the door as soon as she knocked. She wasn't smiling. In fact, her eyes were red and her face blotchy as if she'd been crying. Julia looked questioningly over her head at Sam. He shook his head and shrugged. "I think she's worried that you're taking Lucky away. I tried to reassure her that Lucky would be coming back later, but I guess she doesn't believe me." Julia felt bad for the little girl, but she really did want to bring Lucky along. She bent down and spoke directly to Brinn. "I promise," she said. "I will bring Lucky back before you go to bed, okay?" Brinn stood with her head down, her hand holding Lucky's leash. Without a single word, she handed the leash to Julia, gave Lucky a kiss on the nose and ran into her room. 'Don't worry," said Sam. "She'll be ok. Once we finish our errands and find a place for an ice cream, she'll be fine." Julia was still hesitant. She hated the idea that she was upsetting Brinn this way. "Are you absolutely sure? Because I can leave him if you want." Sam took her by the shoulders and turned her toward the door. "It's fine. Now go, or you won't be back before she goes to bed!" He waved her off with a smile and a thumbs up for good luck. Part of him wanted her trip to be successful, but a small part of him wanted Lucky to become their dog. He knew that wasn't fair. Lucky deserved to be with the people who had raised him and loved him for so long. He knew that was really the best outcome. He sighed. Guess I had better start researching how one goes about adopting a dog. With Brinn showing the attachment she had for Lucky, he knew there was no going back. A dog, whether it was Lucky or some other four footed furry canine, was destined to be in their lives.

Chapter 15

Julia and Lucky pulled off the highway and onto the main street of Wilmot. It was mid morning and things were getting busy. Some people milled about, looking in store windows, strolling leisurely down the street while others bustled along intent on their schedules and appointments. Julia glanced at her map and made the necessary turn that would take her to the local police station. There was a parking area designated for visitors with several empty spaces available. She pulled into one and shut off the engine. She paused for a moment, trying to decide if she should bring Lucky with her right away, or just go on her own and inquire about missing dog reports. She could always come out and get him if anyone wanted to have a better look at him. The day was cold, but she had put an extra blanket on the back seat. Lucky had a thick coat and loved to spend time outdoors in the snow. She was pretty sure that he would be ok in the car for the length of time she would be in the station. She cracked the two front windows open just a bit and turned to speak to Lucky. He was on his feet and looking at her expectantly. "Sorry, buddy," she told him. "you wait here for a few minutes and I'll be right back." The crazy dog seemed to understand. He proceeded to turn himself around a couple of times, bunching up the blankets as he went. When they felt suitably comfortable he flopped down with a huff, as much as to say, "Fine. If that's how you want it. But I don't have to be happy about it!" Julia smiled at his antics and his attitude. "How about we make peace with a couple of treats?" At the word treats, Lucky's head came up and all was forgiven. "Well I'll be darned, " Julia laughed. "The dog speaks English!" She gave Lucky the treats and opened the car door. As she turned to grab her purse and folder, she was nearly bowled over by seventy pounds of dog charging through the car door. "Lucky, no!" she screamed. "Lucky, get back here!" Panic made her heart start to race. Where was he going? He had never jumped out of the car before! "Lucky, come!" She bolted after him, concerned that he might run into the path of an oncoming car. But he wasn't headed for the road. He was headed directly for the front door of the police station. There was a woman coming down the walk. She seemed to be looking for something in her purse, but raised her head when she heard Julia's frantic hollering. When Julia saw that her path and Lucky's were going to intersect, she stopped in mid run. Time started to move in slow motion. Should she call to the woman and ask her to catch the dog? What if she was afraid of dogs? What if Lucky jumped on her or knocked her over? What if he had completely lost his head and decided to attack her? Julia didn't know enough about dogs to know what on earth to expect. All of these thoughts were racing through Julia's head as she waited for the surreal scene to unfold. Lucky did jump on the woman, but instead of being afraid, she was hugging him and petting him and smiling like she had just found her lost best friend!

When time started spinning at a normal rate again, Julia realized that that was exactly what was happening. Except that she kept calling the dog Jasper. Lucky was jumping up and licking her face and she didn't seem the least bit perturbed. Eventually Julia made her way across the parking lot and stood face to face with the mystery woman. She snapped Lucky's leash to his collar, even though he had no intention of going anywhere. Instead he ran from Julia to this other woman and back again as if to say, "Hey you guys. It's about time you found each other!" Julia extended her hand and introduced herself. Wendy did the same. "Do you know this dog?" Julia asked incredulously.

"I do indeed," laughed Wendy. "And you have no idea how happy I am to see him! I was just inside hoping that someone had reported a found dog to the police." It was Julia's turn to laugh. "And I was heading inside to see if anyone had reported a lost dog! Go figure! What do you say we head over to that little café and clear up all the mystery?"

"Sounds good to me," Wendy agreed. Lucky was placed back in Julia's car, under much greater protest this time, and the women headed off to the restaurant. Over steaming cups of coffee, they both retold their stories. At the end of it all, they were both left wondering what to do next. Wendy was going to check with the hospital to see if they would allow Jasper to come in and visit her Dad. Julia agreed to wait in town with Jasper until that could be decided. Then Julia would take Jasper back home for the evening until further arrangements could be made. With her Dad having to remain in hospital, and Wendy being in a "No dogs allowed" hotel, that seemed to be the only solution. With that much decided, Julia returned to the car to wait with Lucky...no, Jasper, while Wendy went in to speak to the hospital staff. At the very least, she would be able to tell her Dad that Jasper had been found, safe and sound.

While Julia appeased Lucky with a few more treats, she began thinking about Sam and Brinn. She was going to have to tell them that Lucky's owners had been found. She hated the thought of breaking Brinn's heart that way. Even though Sam had said they would get another dog, it wouldn't make this parting any easier. No, breaking the news of this was not something she looked forward to at all.

Within minutes Wendy returned to the car and tapped on the driver's side window. Julia got out to speak to her, leaving a very rowdy Jasper jumping from the front seat to the back in an effort to get out. "The hospital has agreed to let me bring Jasper in, but only for a few minutes. Would you like to come in too?" Wendy asked. Julia had to think for a minute. "No, I think this is a special moment for you and your Dad to share. I'm going to quickly go and remove some of the posters we put up nearby, and then I'll just wait here in the parking lot until you bring Luck...Jasper back out." With that, she clipped the leash to Jasper's collar and handed him over to Wendy. "Dad is going to be so happy to see this guy! I can't wait to see his reaction" Julia wished her good luck as she headed off towards the hospital doors. "It's good that someone's going to be happy," she thought to herself. Julia drove a few blocks to the centre of town , stopping here and there where she remembered there being posters. She also stopped quickly at the two animal clinics and the local shelter to let them know that the dog's owners had been located. She did all of this with a heavy heart, for as happy as she was for Lucky, Wendy and the old man, she was equally sad for Brinn and Sam.

For just a brief moment she considered going back to the shelter and surprising Brinn and Sam with the gift of a new dog of their own, but in the end, she decided that that should be a choice for them to make on their own. There was really nothing else she could do, except head back to the hospital, pick up Jasper, and go home and break the news.

Wendy was waiting on a bench outside the hospital as she pulled up. "How did it go?" Julia asked hopefully.

"Really well," Wendy replied. "Dad was so relieved to know that Jasper had been found and taken care of. Are you sure you don't mind taking him back home with you?"

"Not at all," Julia assured her. "Would you like me to bring him back tomorrow?" Wendy thought for a minute and then replied with some hesitation. "Honestly? I don't know what to. The hospital said they would only allow that one visit, so I can't take him in any more. I can't take him to the hotel, and Dad isn't going back to his farm. He will be transferred from the hospital to a long term care facility. I really need some time to think about all of this and make some plans. I know it's a lot to ask, but do you think you could hold onto him for just a few more days until I figure some things out?"

"I'd be happy to. But I should probably tell you that Jasper has been staying with my neighbor for the past few days. I've been crazy busy at work, and he has a little girl who has fallen totally in love with Lucky. They've been having a great time getting to know each other."

"Oh, that's terrific," said Wendy with a smile. "Sounds like they won't mind having their guest for a few more days!"

"Not at all," Julia agreed. "I'll give you my cell number and and you can give me a call whenever you're ready to have me bring Jasper to you." Julia opened the back door for Jasper who jumped rather reluctantly into the back seat. Julia felt sorry for the poor guy. Here he had finally found the people he had loved all his life and now he had to leave them. She sure hoped seeing Brinn again would make it a little easier for him.

Chapter 16

Brinn was watching out her living room window when Julia pulled into the driveway. She was out the door and on Julia's step before the engine stopped running. If she were any other little girl, the running footsteps and happy grin would have been accompanied by shouts of glee and excitement. But Brinn was not any other little girl, and all her happy sounds remained locked inside. Nonetheless, Julia smiled and gave her a big hug. Lucky was wagging from his long snout to the tip of his tail and Julia had to hang on to Brinn to keep her from getting knocked off her feet as he bounded from the car. Brinn knelt down and her arms encircled his neck as he lavished wet slobbery kisses to every skin surface he could find. Julia heart just sank at the thought of how her news was going to affect Brinn. She let them play for a while and then suggested that they go inside. Sam was making his way down the porch to join them, balancing an armful of books and packages. "I just need to put this stuff in my car, and I'll come and get those two out of your hair."

"No hurry. Actually I was hoping you could come inside for a few minutes. I have some news." Sam stopped in his tracks. Julia knew that he knew what was coming. He turned without saying anything, and headed on to his car. "Yep, this is going to be hard," Julia thought once again. Back inside, Julia put a pot of coffee on to brew and dug around in the cupboard for something sweet to serve with it. Brinn was easily distracted from her play outdoors by the promise of cookies, milk and her favorite TV show. With her settled in the living room, Julia and Sam could converse out of earshot. For while there were some definite problems with Brinn's speech, there was absolutely nothing wrong with her hearing, and Sam wanted to be sure she didn't overhear their conversation. He wanted to find out for himself what information Julia had, and to decide how and when to proceed with telling Brinn. Over steaming cups of coffee Julia told Sam exactly how everything had happened. Sam just sat there shaking his head. "What are the odds that all of that would happen?" Then, to quote from one of Brinn's favorite Disney World rides, "Guess it really is a small world after all!" Julia was glad to see that Sam was taking it all pretty good, and without losing his sense of humor. But his hearing the story was the easy part. Telling Brinn was going to be the real challenge. Sam was quiet, then, for a minute or two before he spoke. "So, what happens now? When will you be taking Lucky back?" Julia shook her head and shrugged. "I really don't know for sure. I just said I'd keep him until Wendy phoned me." Sam rubbed the stubble that covered his chin. He obviously hadn't shaved today. Julia was surprised to find how endearing she found that particular habit. In fact, she was kind of surprised at how she was suddenly noticing a lot of things about Sam that she really liked. She wondered if he felt the same way about her. "Julia, get a grip," she admonished herself. "This is not the time." She realized Sam was speaking. "I'm sorry. What was that? " she asked sheepishly. "I was daydreaming."

I'd like to keep Lucky until you get the call," Sam repeated. "If that's ok with you."

"Sure," Julia replied, trying to push her new thoughts about Sam to the back of her mind. "I figured you would want to do that. Are you going to tell Brinn right away or wait till we know when he's leaving?"

"I'm not sure," Sam said with a sadness Julia had never heard before. "I want to think about it for a while before I do anything."

"Well, whatever you do, I know it will be based on what's best for Brinn. I just hope she understands."

"Me too," was all Sam said before rising from the table. He thanked Julia for the coffee and headed to the living room to gather up his little family. "Come on, pipsqueak," he said. "Time for you and your furry sidekick there to get on home. There are chores galore waiting at home with my name written all over them." Julia was impressed at how cheerful he pretended to be, knowing how much he must really be hurting. Yep, he was quite a guy.

Chapter 17

Almost two full days went by before Julia heard back from Wendy. She called late in the evening and asked if Julia could meet her at the hospital the next day. When Julia asked if she should bring Jasper, Wendy was quite emphatic in her denial, saying that the hospital wouldn't let him in again, and that her Dad was getting very agitated by the whole ordeal. "I'll explain everything when I see you, ok?" She seemed to be in quite a state herself, so Julia simply agreed to the meeting and said good-bye. Wendy had sounded completely frazzled and Julia couldn't help but wonder what was going on. "I'll find out soon enough," she thought as she prepared for bed.

She hadn't seen much of Sam or Brinn for the past couple of days. She figured they were spending time together, staying close, and preparing for the heartbreak to come. She wanted to let Sam know she was meeting Wendy, but she didn't want to interrupt them, or have Brinn overhear. She decided just give him a quick call. She dialed his number and she could hear Lucky barking in the background when he answered. "Hi, Sam, It's Julia. Things sound pretty normal over there!"

"Yep, chaos to the max," Sam replied. "What's up?"

"I just wanted to let you know that I'm on my way to meet with Wendy. I don't really have any more information yet, but I wanted you to know."

"Thanks, for letting me know, "Sam said sincerely. "You can fill me in when you get back." Julia said she would and hung up.

Wendy was waiting in her car when Julia arrived. It was a bitter cold day today, so she was keeping the heat on. When she saw Julia pull in, she killed the engine and climbed out. Julia did the same and they met halfway across the lot. "We'd better chat inside," said Wendy. "It's freezing out here!" Julia agreed, although she could see that she was much better prepared for the cold than Wendy was. Julia didn't comment on that but simply said, "Sure, how's the coffee in the hospital cafeteria?" Wendy laughed. "Actually it's better than you might think." They headed in and were soon seated in the warm, almost stuffy cafeteria. The smell of coffee mixed with the ever present underlying smell of antiseptic that all hospitals have. Julia took her coffee black but Wendy was a double, double kind of girl. Julia waited impatiently while she added cream and sugar and then stirred for what seemed like an eternity. Finally she spoke. "Julia, I really want to thank you for taking Lucky in the way you have. If you had turned him over to the shelter, my Dad may have never seen him again. I just want you to know how much I appreciate all you've done." Julia assured her that it had all been a good experience. She explained a little more about Brinn and how wonderful the experience had been for her. "We were really hoping that Lucky might help her to speak again, but no luck so far. Sam plans to get a dog of her own for her once Lucky, I mean Jasper goes home." Wendy had been listening quite intently to Julia's story and Julia noticed that her expression suddenly changed. Instead of looking so desperate and worried, she now looked almost happy, and somewhat expectant. "What is it?" Julia asked. "You look a little like a kid who has discovered that Santa Claus really did come in the night!" Wendy laughed out loud. "You know what? That is kind of how I feel all of a sudden." She paused for a moment, let out a long breath and started in. "I was planning on asking you today if you could keep Jasper permanently, and I was pretty sure that you were going to say no. I tossed and turned all night alternating between arguments to convince you, and alternatives for Jasper. I knew I couldn't take him home, and Dad will be staying here and going into the long term care unit at this hospital. The doctors felt a move across country would be hard on him, and I agreed. That was going to leave Jasper without a home. I hated the thought of handing him over to the shelter now, after all he's been through. But now I think we have the perfect solution!" She relaxed a bit and leaned back in her chair. Julia was quiet. This was not what she had come in here expecting. She had been so sure that Wendy would take the dog with her. She hadn't even thought about the fact that it would have meant moving the dog across country. Was it really possible? Could Lucky really become Brinn's own dog? She just kept staring into her cup and then realized that Wendy was waiting for her to say something. Her silence was obviously bothering her, and she had a worried expression on her face again. Julia looked up and smiled. "Let me get this straight. You want Jasper to stay with my neighbor and his little girl...permanently? As in, be their own dog...for keeps?"

Wendy chuckled. "That's right. What do you think?" There was no long silence this time.

"I think it's a wonderful idea! I can't wait to get home and tell Sam! Brinn is going to be over the moon!"

"There's just one more little thing," Wendy said with a bit of hesitation. "Do you think, once my dad is settled, that you could bring Jasper by once and a while to see him? There is a family lounge in the center where therapy animals are often brought in for visits. If Jasper has all his shots and is brought in with a registered guest, he can visit there any time."

"That would be no problem at all," Julia replied emphatically. "Jasper really is a therapy dog. He has been for Brinn and now he can be for your Dad too! I think this is all going to work out fine!"

The women finished their coffees, chatted about jobs, homes, and kids before rising to leave. Julia started donning all of her winter gear and Wendy threw her coat over her arm. She was heading back upstairs to visit her Dad before heading out to his farm to take care of things there. They agreed to talk again in the morning to make any final arrangements, and to make sure that nothing about their plans had changed. Julia was almost positive that Sam would be in agreement, but she didn't want to make any guarantees until she had at least spoken to him. The women parted ways at the door, each with their own thoughts focused on things that would be changing in the very near future.

Chapter 18

Julia couldn't drive home fast enough. She smiled to herself thinking, "If ever there was a day that I was going to get a speeding ticket, this would be it." She was so anxious to get home and tell Sam the news. She sure hoped he would be as excited as she was. She also really, really hoped that he hadn't yet talked to Brinn about having to give Lucky up. All the more reason to hurry home. She pushed the accelerator just a little bit harder. Thank goodness there hadn't been any more snow, and the roads were dry. Just a couple more miles, and she could deliver some really good news to some really good friends.

When she pulled in the drive, she was disappointed to see that Sam's car wasn't in the driveway. "Darn," she muttered under her breath. "Now I'm going to have to wait till they get home." A few minutes later she had a second thought. Maybe their not being home was a good thing. Julia decided she would make the most of the opportunity and throw an impromptu welcome home party for Jasper. She would tie some bows to the verandah, print off a quick banner on her computer, and fix a big thermos of hot chocolate, complete with marshmallows and whipped cream. She still had some special treats for Jasper, and maybe she would even indulge him with one of the oatmeal cookies she was going to serve with the hot chocolate. She thought it would be a great way to break the news to Sam, although she supposed he might not get it at first. On second thought, she knew Sam was a pretty smart fellow. He would probably be able to guess what it meant. At any rate, to Julia, it sounded like fun. She got right to work making the banner, and while it was printing, she dug up some holiday ribbon for the porch. She also found some balloons left over from a recent open house, and she blew those up as well. Within about fifteen minutes the house looked as though there was big celebration going on. Once the decorating was taken care of, Julia set to work making the hot chocolate and arranging the cookies.

She was so engrossed in her plans, she didn't hear Sam's car pull in. The first indication she had that they were home, was Jasper barking in the yard. When she went to the front window to look out, she could see Brinn grinning and pointing to the decorations. She was tugging on Sam's arm for all she was worth trying to hurry him to Julia's door. Sam was reluctant at first, thinking that Julia maybe had a party for clients or friends happening, and he didn't want to intrude. Sometimes sharing a duplex, and being friends created a sense of being quite at home in either place for Brinn. The last thing Sam wanted to do was intrude on Julia's privacy. But then he looked up and saw the banner. "Welcome home Jasper!" it read.

It took only a few seconds for the meaning to hit him, and he sure hoped he was right. Now he hurried to follow Brinn's lead. Julia opened the door before they hit the second step. She was grinning from ear to ear. Sam couldn't hold back. "Does that mean what I think it means?" he asked.

"You bet it does." "If you want him he's yours!"

"If we want him? If we want him" Did you hear that Brinn? He picked up the little girl and swung her around. Lucky is going to stay with us forever! We may have to start calling him Jasper, because that's his real name but he's going to be our dog. Our dog for keeps!"

Jasper was barking and spinning around like a mad dog. He was making so much noise, that they almost missed the tiny voice that surfaced through the chaos.

"Jasper, my doggy," said Brinn. "My doggy for keeps." Sam stopped his crazy waltz and stared into the eyes of the little girl he loved more than life itself. He was overcome at the sound of the voice he hadn't heard in over a year. Tears welled up in his eyes as he hugged her even closer. Julia bent down to calm Jasper while trying to get control of the tears that filled her own. Jasper licked her face and ran back to Brinn. Sam set her down and she hugged

Jasper with the kind of affection that kids and dogs seem to find so effortless.

"Jasper, my doggy," she repeated into his ear. "My doggy for keeps!"

Epilogue

It is a beautiful warm spring day in Lilac Creek. The flowers for which the town is named are in full bloom, their heady aroma filling the air. A young couple sit on a bench in a courtyard outside the Wilmot Hospital. They are holding hands and smiling, their eyes focused on another area of the garden a few feet away. Under the purple haze of a huge lilac bush, sits an old man in a wheelchair. At his feet sits a little brown haired girl in blue jeans and a red sweater. She is chattering away, nonstop, telling him all about a new friend that she has made at daycare. The old man smiles and nods, for he only speaks occasionally. He understands very well, however, and he is totally bewitched by his little friend. He keeps one hand resting gently on the head of a furry brown and tan mutt who sits on the other side of his chair. The dog keeps a close protective eye on the little girl. His eyes move back and forth between the girl and the old man. When his eyes meet the old man's a look of complete understanding passes between them. The dog knows he is totally loved by both man and girl, and gives mountains of unconditional love to both in return, and will continue to do so for as long as he lives. "For keeps."

The end

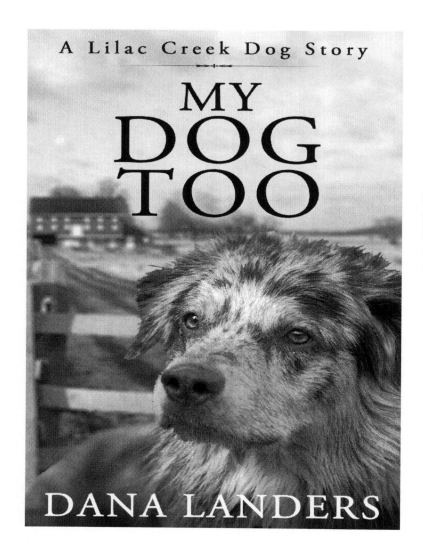

A Lilac Creek Dog Story

MY DOG TOO

DANA LANDERS

My Dog Too

Prologue

She would definitely have to be more careful going out during the day. If someone saw her, it would ruin everything. But she had been so hungry, and the small apple tree laden with unpicked fruit had been too hard to resist. Since it was just barely past dawn, she was pretty sure no one would have seen her. She settled herself back into a corner of the loft where there was a good view of the farmhouse through a crack in the old boards of the barn. When she had come across the unoccupied farm two days ago, she had decided the old barn was the perfect place to hide for a few days while she made her plan. But there was a family living here now and that changed everything.

Emma figured that the people who now lived in the house must be the new owners. She had secretly watched as two men unloaded boxes and furniture from a small moving van the day before and there was now a stack of broken down boxes sitting to one side of the porch. All day yesterday Emma had stayed quiet and hidden while the commotion of moving took place. She was so afraid that the movers would be bringing items to store in the old barn. But everything had been unloaded into the house and the garage, so she felt secure and safe in her little hideout. In the few chances she took to watch the goings on, she had seen a little girl a few years younger than herself, and a brown scruffy mutt that seemed to be glued to her side everywhere she went. There had been a man and a woman as well, but Emma had only had glimpses of them as they went from the truck to the house. Today would be for watching, waiting and learning more about this new family.

Chapter 1

It was an unusually warm day for the end of October, and everyone was taking advantage of it, knowing that the first snowfall could arrive at any time. This was probably the only time of the year that wasn't really spectacular in Lilac Creek. The blaze of fall color was gone and the dazzling white of winter had not yet arrived. The fragrance and purple haze of spring lilacs were a distant memory, as were the lush green woodlands and sparkling blue waters of summer. This was what Julia often called the "grey" season.

But in today's unusually warm sun, she sat on the front porch absently rubbing the melon that was now her belly, reflecting on how much her life had changed in the past two years. Back then, her world revolved around her work, with what spare time she did have going to renovations on the house. Now here she was, seven months pregnant, watching her five year old daughter playing in the yard with her husband Sam, and their adopted dog Jasper! Julia was still amazed at how quickly she had grown to love the big brown mutt that had come so unexpectedly into her life. And becoming a wife and mother had been the icing on the cake. Yes, life was good, indeed, but even more changes were in store, one of the biggest ones being their move to the farm. Tomorrow they would move from their cozy little duplex to the big old farmhouse previously owned by Henry Thompson, Jasper's original owner.

Since he was living permanently at the long term care centre, his daughter Wendy had decided it was time to sell his farm. She had naturally contacted Julia, Lilac Creek's main realtor. Julia had taken several trips out to the property and she and Sam had gone through the old house thoroughly in preparation for listing it on the market. On one of those trips, it suddenly hit Julia that this could be just the place for her growing family. They had been discussing moving to a bigger place for some time but nothing that really struck them had come onto the market lately. It was well into fall and not a time when most folks wanted to move, since school had already begun for the new term.

But as Julia wandered through the house on one particular visit, everything just seemed to click into place. There were four bedrooms upstairs, a big open kitchen and a large living room dining room combination on the main level. Another couple of rooms off the living room would serve nicely as a family room and an office, so Julia could work from home once the baby arrived. She and Sam had discussed it at length and when they asked Brinn for her opinion, she was over the moon with excitement. Living on a farm seemed to her to be about the best idea in the world, and the fact that Jasper would be moving back to his original home made it seem just perfect. And now, their cozy little house was almost all packed up and ready for the move.

After a while, Sam, Brinn and Jasper joined her on the porch for a rest. Jasper might be getting on in years, but his energy level was quite incredible. Both Sam and Brinn were still trying to catch their breath. "I swear that dog could run all day!" sighed Sam as he fell into the chair beside Julia. Brinn was sprawled on the porch beside Jasper, nose to nose, one arm around his scruff as she had always done from the first day they met. Julia was certain the dog could read Brinn's mind, they were so in tune with each other. She marveled at the changes that the last two years had meant for Brinn. She had gone from a traumatized preschooler who wouldn't speak, to a thriving five year old with a contagious love for life that rubbed off on everyone she met. Her adopted dog Jasper had been the catalyst for that remarkable recovery and Julia thanked her lucky stars every day for his constant devotion. Jasper had changed all of their lives in so many ways.

Once they had rested a bit, Sam suggested that they head inside to wash up and get changed. "Since the kitchen is all packed up and the movers are coming early in the morning, how about I take my favorite ladies out for supper?" When Jasper woofed, everyone laughed and Sam agreed that his favorite furry gentleman could come too. "I know you think you're a person," Sam laughed as he rubbed Jasper's head, but you'll have to wait in the car, I'm afraid!" As if he understood, Jasper began spinning in circles and barking. He didn't care what he had to do as long as he got to go along!

Chapter 2

Brinn was so excited she could barely sit still. She was sitting in the middle of the living room floor surrounded by boxes and furniture, throwing a tennis ball for Jasper down the empty space in the middle of the room. As usual Jasper was running full tilt after the ball with little consideration for the fact that all of the rugs had been rolled up and the hardwood floors were like a big skating rink. Each time he tried to run he did an award winning imitation of Bambi first discovering ice. But it didn't slow him down. Each time he would scramble till his feet found purchase and then slide into the wall at the other end to capture his prize. As comical as the routine was, Brinn hardly noticed. All she could think about was getting out to the farm and discovering all the great new adventures just waiting for her there.

This was the first move that she was really old enough to be excited about. She had been too young to remember their move to Lilac Creek. All she really remembered from that move was an overwhelming sense of sadness because Mommy wasn't coming with them. At first, unable to accept the reality of losing her Mom, she remained silent and steadfast in her belief that her Mom had simply stayed behind at their old house, and that she would join them soon. Eventually, the love and patience of a devoted father helped her remember just why her Mom was not with them, and to accept their new situation. For a long time she was unable to talk about it, but Jasper had changed all that. He had become her loving protector and faithful companion, helping her become once again the cheerful little girl she had been before. And now they were going to live in the house where Jasper used to live and to Brinn that was like a miracle. Brinn tossed the tennis ball once again down their makeshift alleyway, but instead of going after it, Jasper ran in the completely opposite direction barking wildly.

"The movers are here!" Brinn shouted, jumping up to follow behind the crazed Jasper. "Yay! It's time to go!" Brinn followed Jasper to the window where they could watch what was going on but not be in the way. Brinn could see her Mom and Dad talking to the moving men as they opened the huge back door of the truck. She continued to watch with amazement as they unfolded a long ramp that extended from the back of the truck, across the porch stairs and right up to the front door. It looked like a little bridge and Brinn thought it would be lots of fun to play on. But she knew she was supposed to stay out of the way so she had to be content with just watching.

Once the truck and ramp were in place, the movers and her parents came inside to plan out the loading of the truck. Always his jovial friendly self, Jasper circled their legs and wagged his bushy tail as if they were his long lost friends. Each of the movers scratched his ears just as he was hoping they would and then continued with the task at hand. When Sam and the movers headed upstairs so they could see what they had to pack from those rooms, Julia called Brinn and Jasper into the kitchen. "I need you to pack up the bag of toys that you kept out for today, along with Jasper's things, "she said. "We're going to head out to the farm now so we can get things opened up and ready for the movers when they arrive."

"Okay," replied Brinn without hesitation. She was ready to get out to the farm and start exploring the new surroundings. She quickly threw all of her things into her backpack and stuffed Jasper's tennis balls, dishes, chew toys and blanket into another bag. She met her Mom at the car and climbed into her booster seat in the back. Jasper hopped in beside her, curling his big body as best he could to fit the confined space. Julia placed a few last items that they had used for breakfast into the trunk and slammed it closed.

As she started to back down the driveway, the full impact of leaving the very first home she had bought suddenly hit her. She had spent hours and hours on all the renovations and landscaping, and every single one of those undertakings was a labor of love. She had turned the rather run down property into a cozy welcoming home, one that she had shared with an amazing man who had first been a kind, caring neighbor, and who was now her husband.

When she looked at the garden she could picture Brinn sitting there playing, silent and sad in her grief, until Jasper licked her face one day and turned her whole upside down world back right again. She thought back on the small wedding ceremony they had held right there in this same garden with just a few close friends and family. She could almost smell the lilacs that were in full bloom, and she could see Brinn walking down the path in her lavender dress, Jasper at her side, a big purple bow around his neck. Jasper had been the perfect gentleman, sitting proud and still beside his little girl all through the ceremony. She smiled then, remembering what had finally made him come undone. Just as the minister introduced them as the new Mr. and Mrs. Sam Baxter, a small red squirrel had run across the top of the garden fence right under Jasper's nose. He had taken off in hot pursuit, through the gate and out into the garden. No harm was done and everyone agreed that he had already surpassed all expectations of good dog behavior and cheered him on. The squirrel eventually disappeared up an old oak tree and out of sight. Jasper returned to the group with a "mission accomplished" grin on his furry face.

Julia was completely swamped by the flood of memories that just kept coming. Only the insistent voice in the back seat brought her back into the realm of reality. "Mommy! Are we going now?" Judging by her tone, Julia figured Brinn had probably asked her a number of times already.

"Yes, love, we're going now." Julia started the car moving again. She and Sam would come back tomorrow for a final walkthrough of the duplex. She would say her final goodbyes then. Happy to be on the move finally, Brinn settled in to talk to Jasper about the excitement that lay ahead. She told him all about how he was going back to the farm where he used to live, and how they were going to fix it all up and make it their own house. Busy with her conversation, she was occupied for the whole trip out to the farm.

As they approached the turnoff to the country road leading to the farm, Jasper began to get very restless. He started to whine and yip in the back seat, standing up to look out the window as they drove.

The big bushy tail started to wave back and forth, and had Brinn not been in the seat beside him, Julia is certain he would have started pacing back and forth from window to window. The whining turned into a full fledged bark when they turned into the long laneway leading to the house. "I think he recognizes this place, "Julia said to Brinn who was concerned by Jasper's erratic behavior. "He remembers that this is where he used to live." It was all they could do to keep Jasper from climbing over top of Brinn to get out once they stopped the car. A stern "Wait!" from Julia calmed him down while she got Brinn safely out of his way. Once he got the go ahead signal, he bounded out of the back seat and started running frantically around the yard. He ran and sniffed every corner of the garden and then stood anxiously by the door waiting for Julia to undo the lock. As she pushed the door open, Jasper bolted inside running from room to room, nose sniffing and tail wagging. Brinn was jumping up and down and following him all around, completely caught up in the excitement. But Julia saw his excitement for what it really was and her heart went out to the furry mutt.

Before long the frantic sniffing from room to room slowed down, and the excited bark became more of a whimper. Having sniffed out every corner of the house, he turned his big brown eyes to Julia and she could see the question there.

"Where is he?" Julia was certain he was asking. "I thought Henry would be here," he seemed to be saying. Julia bent down to ruffle his long fur.

"I know, Bud," she said softly. "You thought he would be here didn't you?" In all the excitement over moving, she hadn't even thought about this maybe happening, that Jasper would expect the old man to be there. How was a dog supposed to remember that the man who had loved him and raised him for so many years wasn't there anymore? Jasper had just blended into their lives so easily that they sometimes forgot he hadn't been theirs forever. Julia continued to stroke the furry head and show him as much love as she could. She knew in time, Jasper would accept that while this was the house where he and Henry had lived, that Henry himself was no longer there. Julia made a mental note to take Jasper for a visit to see Henry at the hospital as soon as they got settled in. In the meantime, there was a lot of work to be done to get to that point. Thinking that Jasper was likely responding to her feelings as much as anything else, Julia changed her tone and offered Jasper one of the treats from his bag. He responded readily and the next thing she knew he and Brinn were off looking for secret hideaways that somehow Brinn had convinced herself came with the house.

Sam and the movers arrived a few hours later and the rest of the day was spent getting everything moved into the house. A chilly October rain had begun to fall so they tried to hurry things along. Once the moving van was unloaded, the big truck pulled away and the family was left on their own. Brinn was disappointed that the rain kept them from doing much exploring outside but she and Jasper ran from empty room to empty room imagining all the many ways they were going to enjoy their new space. Before long, night had fallen and the darkness of the country property felt strange and a little bit scary to Brinn. They lit a warm fire in the fireplace and gathered around it, exhausted from the long day. Jasper and Brinn curled up together on a big blanket in front of the fire and quickly fell asleep.

Chapter 3

Emma knew the people in the house were up and about now because soft light filtered through the lacy curtains. She could hear sounds of someone clanking dishes in the kitchen, but she was too far away to hear any voices. Suddenly someone opened the screen door and the big brown and black dog she had seen yesterday came bounding out, ready for play after his night inside. The dog was about the size of the golden retriever she remembered from her last school where he was a guide dog for a little blind girl. This dog wasn't golden at all though, but mostly brown with some black and tan on his legs and haunches. He had a big scruffy collar and ears that looked as though they couldn't decide whether to stand up or fall down. He appeared to have a perpetual smile on his face as he charged about, his tail waving like a banner as he ran. Emma wanted so badly to go and run with him, have him jump beside her as he waited impatiently for her to throw a stick. She wanted nothing more than to run through this meadow with that dog at her heels discovering all kinds of treasures along the way. He continued to race about for a while and then settled down to the serious business of sniffing around. Nose to the ground, he became intent on identifying every creature that had passed through the property the night before.

Suddenly Emma froze. What if he could smell her? What if he stood at the door to the old barn and started barking to alert the new owners to a stranger in the loft? Emma remembered reading once about how powerful a dog's sense of smell was, and that they could tell everything about a friend or foe by sniffing where they had been. Instinctively, Emma pulled herself into a ball and stayed very still. She scrunched her eyes closed and willed the dog to go away. After a time, he did just that. Emma allowed herself to breathe normally again but she remained absolutely still. Staying out of sight of people was one thing, but avoiding a big, curious dog was quite another matter.

After a time, the screen door opened again and a woman appeared with a large stainless steel bowl. She sat the bowl down in a corner of the porch and within seconds the dog came running from clear across the yard to devour its contents. Emma smiled along with the woman who gave the dog's ears a scratch before turning around and heading inside. Emma thought she looked like a really nice, happy lady. Her hair was pulled back in a ponytail that poked through the back of a faded blue ball cap, and her oversized gray sweatshirt said "Big Dog" in bold letters across the front. From her secret spot in the loft, Emma watched the proceedings with a big smile on her face and a deep sense of longing in her heart. She didn't know why, but something inside told her this lady was a person she would like to have as a friend. As she walked away the lady waved a finger lovingly at the big mutt. "Now don't gobble!" she said laughingly. Emma remembered how her dog Tucker had always gobbled down his food like it was the last meal he was ever going to have. She remembered how her mother used to say "Now, Tucker, don't gobble." It never mattered. Tucker gobbled every time. But that was a long time ago. Emma felt that old familiar tug in her heart.

She had only been four the last time she and her parents had been together, but she had deep rooted memories of those happy times. Her parents, their cabin and Tucker had been her whole world. Neither of her parents had any other family and there were no neighbors nearby. Her parents had chosen the small cabin at the edge of the woods for the solitude it would provide. Although the cabin had been small, Emma remembered it always being cozy and inviting. There was a large second cabin on the property that had served as a workplace for both her parents. It was just one big open space with a big stone fireplace that took up one entire wall. Her father had set up an office in one corner for his writing, and her mom had claimed the rest of the space as a studio where she created magnificent paintings. Emma could remember spending her days playing on the rug in front of the fire. She and Tucker would play there for hours while her parents worked. There was a big basket of toys on each side of the fireplace, one for her and one for Tucker. He would lie beside her chewing one of his squeaky toys while she played with her dolls or her stuffed animals. Somehow he would always sense when she was growing bored with what she was doing, and right then he would get up and dig through his toy basket for a ball or a stick. He would bring it over to her and drop it in her lap as much as to say, "Ok, now it's time to play." Emma would get her outdoor clothes on and out they'd go. Her Mom would always have a snack ready for her when they came back in.

She closed her eyes as she sat in the old deserted loft and remembered those happy days. But things were different now. In one split second her happy world had been shattered and everything she held dear had been taken from her. Now she was on her own, completely alone, but thankful for her treasured memories and this deserted barn that for now would provide her with the shelter she needed and the freedom she so desperately wanted.

At last, with his belly full and his morning routines completed, the big dog flopped onto the wooden floor of the porch, claiming a big sun drenched space for his very own. Emma's fingers almost itched with a desire to bury her face in the silky fur and breathe in that soothing aroma of warm dog.

But Emma knew she had to stay hidden. No matter how nice that lady might seem, if she found Emma hiding in her barn, she would have to go back to another foster home. Emma just didn't think she could stand that again.

She was so confused. She didn't really know where she planned to go, but something in her heart kept pulling her towards her old home. Although sensibility tried to niggle its way to the front of her thinking, Emma squashed it down and told herself that if she could just make it back to their old cabin she could be happy. Maybe, she thought, no one had moved into their cabin. Maybe, even if someone had, there was a chance they wouldn't be using the workshop. She could set up a little home for herself there. And in weaving her web of dreams, she imagined that maybe Tucker was still living there too. No one had ever told her what really happened to Tucker when they came to take her away from her home. All the lady who picked her up said was that he would be taken care of.

At the time, there was nothing Emma could do but go along. Her parents were gone, she had to go live with strangers, and she never saw Tucker again. In her fantasy, Tucker would be there waiting for her when she finally made her way home. They would hide out together in the cozy workshop and be happy forever. All she had to do was get there.

But for now she had to concentrate on staying hidden while she made her plan. She scooted back into the shadows of the barn's loft and settled herself into the little bed that she had made by scraping some loose straw together into a pile. She could hear voices coming from the farmhouse, but she didn't want to risk moving around in case they headed her way.

After a time, she also heard doors slamming and car engines starting. Knowing that they were all near the driveway, Emma chanced a glimpse out the little crack that served as her window on the world. The nice lady was leaving in the little car, and the man, the dog and the little girl were all in the truck. Emma was surprised at the sudden feeling of loneliness that came over her at the thought that they were all leaving. She had been comforted knowing they were around even though they were totally unaware of her presence.

After a few minutes, though, she realized that maybe this would be the perfect opportunity to sneak inside and borrow a few supplies for her journey, and some food for her rumbling belly. She really hoped that the door wouldn't be locked. She felt a little pang of guilt as she contemplated taking things that weren't hers for the taking, but she really only needed a little food and maybe another warm blanket or two.

Emma waited for a few minutes to make sure both car and truck were not coming back for some reason, and then she scooted over to the rickety old ladder and climbed carefully down. She crouched low as she made her way across the lawn to the house even though she knew the people inside were gone. It was almost a habit now, to stay low and stay quiet. She moved quickly, not wanting to chance being out in the open if someone came by. She crossed the wide plank floor of the porch and held her breath as she turned the old wobbly door knob. The door was a bit sticky, but it wasn't locked and it pushed open with a creak and a groan. Emma left the door standing open as she slowly entered the mud room off the kitchen. There were still boxes piled everywhere and she had to weave her way through them. She finally came into the bright sunlit kitchen. The paint was faded but a bright checkered cloth adorned the round table and a big bowl of fruit in the middle made her mouth start to water. She peeked into the fridge and helped herself to two bottles of water from the dozen or so that were there. She really didn't think anyone would miss them. She added a container of yogurt and a bagel to the water and sat everything on the table beside the fruit bowl then went to continue her search for something to help her stay warm at night. There was a big fluffy blanket on the floor in front of the fireplace, but Emma knew that taking it would be too obvious. Instead, she retreated back to the mud room where she had seen several old wooden shelves loaded with all kinds of stuff. From the haphazard way things were piled on the shelves and the dust that had settled on most of them, Emma decided that they must be things left behind by the previous owners. If that was the case, she figured the new owners wouldn't even know she had taken anything. She quickly scanned the items and was excited to find an old flannel sleeping bag rolled up in one corner. She pulled it down and undid the straps. The long tube of sleeping bag would work as a sack to carry her supplies back to the loft. She quickly stuffed a second blanket and an old knitted sweater into the makeshift bag and headed back to the kitchen.

There, she put the two water bottles, yogurt and bagel into the bag along with an apple and an orange. She really wanted the banana that was there too, but there was only one and she thought someone might notice if it was gone. Hoisting the sack over her shoulder, Emma took one last quick look around the mud room. She would love to have some warmer boots and socks, but it didn't seem like there was anything like that around. She decided that what she had found on this trip would do for now, and she was starting to get a little nervous about being in the house so long. She pulled the old creaky door shut behind her as she headed back to her little safe haven in the loft, her mind happy with the thought of some yummy snacks and a warmer night's sleep.

Chapter 4

In town, Julia quickly finished up her errands. She wanted to get
back to the farm and get some more unpacking and organizing
done. Sam had taken Brinn and Jasper to the playground to give
her a bit of time to work without any distractions. They would only
be gone a while and Julia really hoped that would give her time to
at least get the kitchen unpacked. The trip into town had already
eaten up some of that time but she had desperately needed some
cleaning supplies and storage bins to do justice to the long
neglected kitchen cupboards. So it was with some impatience that
she answered the greeting from an acquaintance as she left the
grocery store.

"Julia! Nice to see you." The voice came from the car two spaces
over. It was Carol Lindstrom. Carol was well known in Lilac Creek
as "The Foster Mom" to several kids of varying ages. Julia didn't
know her well, but had met one little girl in her care who was a
friend of Brinn's. They had exchanged pleasantries at several
birthday parties and soccer games.

"Oh, hi, Carol," Julia said, shoving a very huge bag of dog kibble into
the very small trunk of her car. "Shopping for all those hungry
mouths you have to feed?"

"As always!" answered Carol with a small smile and a shrug. "But
have you heard the latest? We have one less mouth to feed right
now."

"No, I hadn't heard," said Julia as she slammed the trunk closed.
"Did one of your kids go back home?"

"I wish it were that simple! No, our most recent and most short
staying member, Emma, just up and ran away. The Sherriff has
been by and everyone's looking for her, but no news yet. Greg and I
feel just awful."

"Don't be too hard on yourself," Julia offered supportively. "You know better than anyone how these kids can just get an idea in their head and run with it. No doubt she'll turn up at a friends' house or the local drop in centre."

"Ya, I hope you're right," Carol said and shrugged again. "Anyway, keep your eyes peeled for a brown haired, brown eyed dynamo about four and half feet tall. She's a real firecracker and not the least bit afraid of being on her own. If she has decided to head out of town she might very well wander by your new place. How is the move going by the way?"

"We're getting there, slowly but surely," Julia replied thinking to herself how fast news travels in a small town like Lilac Creek.

"I'll keep an eye out for Emma," Julia assured her, wondering what would make a ten year old little girl prefer to be on her own instead of in the care of a couple who seemed as caring as Carol and Greg. Just the thought of a lonely little girl out in the world all alone made her remember how sad Brinn had been when they first met. But not anymore. Jasper had changed all of that. Julia imagined for a moment that maybe, if Emma did happen by their new place, that one big slobbery kiss from Jasper could be just the thing to help her too!

Julia's imagination started painting a picture of Brinn and an older sister running through the fields around the old farm with a barking Jasper leading the way. She herself would be sitting on the big verandah in a creaky wooden rocker watching them play as she cradled their new little baby in her arms. Eventually they would all congregate on the porch for cold drinks and snacks, each one, including the dog, taking turns kissing those chubby baby cheeks.

Julia couldn't help but laugh at herself and her vivid imagination. Giving her head a little shake, she returned to her thoughts of cupboard cleaning and unpacking. Armed with all her supplies, Julia headed for home. It still amazed her every time she made the trip to and from town that they now owned a big old house in the country! When she had bought the duplex in town she was certain that she would never leave, or ever be able to love another house as much as she loved that place. But life really has a way of upsetting the apple cart! Now here she was married to a fantastic man with a five year old daughter and another baby on the way, all because her car one wintery day decided to collide with a big brown and tan mutt named Jasper. As if on cue, Jasper came running down the lane at the sound of her car approaching.

"Well I guess I didn't beat them home," thought Julia to herself and smiling at the fur ball flying towards her. She slowed the car to a crawl so she could keep an eye on him, and pulled carefully into her parking spot. Jasper was still barking and his ruckus had Brinn and Sam both coming out of the house to see what was going on.

"No fear of arriving unnoticed is there?" she directed at Sam.

"Not a chance!" he laughed as he started helping her unload the bags in the back seat. "If you were hoping for an element of surprise, you were definitely barking up the wrong tree! Pardon the pun, I couldn't resist!" They both laughed and headed for the house, watching Jasper change his focus immediately to Brinn when he saw her come out of the house.

"Can I stay outside with Jasper?" asked Brinn."We'll just play in the meadow." Julia looked to Sam who glanced around the wide expanse of yard bordered by the much thicker brush and forest.

"You can play here in the open areas," said Sam as he gestured to the grassy area between the house and the old barn. "Don't go into the woods or behind the barn. Stay where your Mom and I can see you from the house, ok?"

"Ok," replied Brinn. She loved being outside and to her the whole world was full of possibilities of adventure. With Jasper at her side, they were an invincible pair and without a bit of direction, they would go anywhere, try anything. They headed happily off to investigate the abandoned vegetable garden where her Mom had said they might find some carrots or squash still good for eating.

After pulling up a few remaining carrots from the garden, Brinn quickly became distracted by the little stream that flowed past the garden in behind the old barn and off into the woods. The water was crystal clear and Jasper didn't hesitate to jump in. Because she hadn't thought to put her rubber boots on, Brinn remained on shore, laughing as Jasper tried to unearth big rocks from the bottom of the stream. He would find one that he liked, dig at it for a while and then dive his nose in to try and remove it. He didn't really like having his head under the water, though, so he would come up snorting and snuffling with water flying everywhere as he shook. Then he'd take a couple breaths and repeat the whole act all over again, each time with lots of yipping and yapping. Brinn laughed at his antics and cheered him on. "Isn't this fun, Jasper?" she squealed. "I knew we would have tons of adventures here on the farm!" When they tired of that game, Brinn found a big gnarled stick and started tossing it for Jasper to catch. Giving it all she had, Brinn threw the stick out into the open meadow. Several times Jasper chased it and brought it back. Then he got distracted by a flock of geese flying overhead and wasn't looking when Brinn made a long and hard throw in the direction of the old barn. When Jasper turned to her again the stick was already long gone and he had no idea which direction to go. Looking at her with a big goofy dog expression, Jasper just stood there waiting. "Well come on then," said Brinn. "We have to go find it." As she headed out into the meadow Jasper barked his approval.

The sound of a dog barking very nearby roused Emma from her daydreams. She stole a quick peek through the cracks in the siding of the barn. She could see the little girl and the dog moving closer as they played in the stream. Her heart started to race and she could feel it pounding in her ears. What if the dog smelled her? What if they came into the barn and found her? Emma held her breath and stayed very still. She was holding all her muscles so tight they were starting to tremble. Now the little girl and the dog were right under the spot where Emma had been watching them. The little girl was laughing and talking to the dog as they passed by. "I threw it right over here! Didn't you watch where it went?" The dog barked loudly and Emma held her breath. She was sure he had caught her scent and was trying to let the little girl know! But the girl simply ignored his barking as she kicked aside the long brown grass. After a few moments she bent down and retrieved the knobby old stick that the dog had been chasing. She waved it over her head, and teasingly called to the big dog. "Here it is Jasper! I found it!" At the sight of his refound treasure, the big dog began jumping up and barking for the game to continue. The girl threw the stick back towards the house, and then continued to walk in that direction herself. As the distance between them and the barn increased, Emma slowly began to relax. She silently released the breath she'd been holding and crept up to peer through the crack. The dog and his little companion were now back at the house. The little girl perched on the porch steps while the dog took a long drink from a big stainless steel bowl. When he was done, he sprawled out at the girl's feet, ready for the next round of play as soon as she made the move. They spent the remainder of the afternoon alternating between exploratory trips to the meadow and playing hide and seek in the small orchard that grew off to one side of the property. The trees were small and had branches low to the ground just perfect for climbing, but Brinn wasn't quite tall enough to get all the way into the crook of the first branch. She settled instead, for picking a few of the last remaining apples to take home to her Mom. She had just picked the last of what she could carry when she heard her Mom calling her in for supper.

The days were getting a lot shorter now and the rest of her play time would have to be saved for indoors. But Brinn loved her new big room with the window that looked out over the meadow and she still had all her boxes of toys to unpack and arrange on her shelves. She called to Jasper and skipped all the way back to the house, the big brown dog never leaving her side.

Chapter 5

The nights were definitely starting to get colder and Emma was so glad that she had some warmer blankets and the warm sweater she had found. She so wished that she had a flashlight or some kind of lantern for the night time, but she hadn't been been able to find anything when she was in the house that morning. At times she could hear small rustling noises in other parts of the barn and she really wished she could see what was making them when they came too close. For the most part though, the old abandoned barn was quiet, relatively warm, and for now, at least, safe.

Through the long dark night Emma dreamt that she was back at her cabin feeding chocolate cake to Tucker while her Mom and Dad sat and chatted by the big fireplace. It was a happy dream and the warm feeling stayed with her as she opened her eyes to a new day. Then she remembered. She wasn't at home. She wasn't even at the Lindstrom's anymore. She was here in this old abandoned barn, all alone and only able to watch the happy family who lived here from her secret hiding place. She couldn't even pet the awesome dog that lived there. She couldn't take the chance that she might be discovered. The reality of being so completely alone banished the warm memories of her dream in an instant. But Emma was not prone to feeling sorry for herself. Her Mom used to tell her that feeling sorry for yourself was nothing but a waste of time, and that if something was making you sad, then it was best to tackle it head on and look for a solution. So that was what Emma was going to do. Today she would start making plans for her future.

First, she would need to consider her options. Now that she had made the decision to run away, she wasn't really sure what her next step should be. All she could think about was getting back home, to be somewhere familiar, to maybe find some thread from her past that she could use to weave together a new life. But suddenly that option seemed so impossible. There would most likely be new people living in their cabin. Tucker was probably already happy in some new place and there wasn't anyone special from her old life that she could contact for help. So maybe that whole idea was a waste of time after all. She supposed that she could try to stay here and stay hidden in this old barn. If she were very careful, she could continue to sneak into the house for food and supplies. She could use the tiny stream that ran through the property to stay clean, and maybe she would even eventually make friends with the big dog without the family even finding out. She had all of the woods and meadows around the farm to explore when the family was gone for the day. If she was very, very careful, Emma thought, she could maybe even spend time indoors during their absence to watch a bit of television and maybe even cook some warm food for herself. She didn't really like the idea of stealing from the nice people, who lived here, but somehow it didn't really feel like stealing since she was only taking what she needed to survive, and she only took things that she thought they would never miss anyway.

As she let those plans roll around in her head, Emma started to feel pretty excited. Maybe this could work out after all! All she had to do was be really really careful and everything would be fine. Feeling almost happy for the first time in weeks, Emma took the pencil and notepad from her backpack and started making her list.

First on the list was another warm blanket. The nights were really starting to get cold. Second was maybe some warmer clothes if she could find something to fit. The lady who lived in the house was pretty tiny, and the little girl was only a bit smaller than she was, so that shouldn't be a problem. Some boots would be nice too, for doing her exploring. Emma hoped there would be an extra pair of rubber boots like those that always stayed on the mat outside the front door around somewhere that no one wore anymore. She remembered how her mom had always had extra boots in the storage room that she kept "just in case" after she bought new ones. Maybe, Emma thought, if I can find a storage room like that inside, I'll be able to find everything I need without anyone ever noticing.

For the rest of the day Emma busied herself with plans for making the old dusty loft her new home. She finished up the rest of the food she had found that morning, and tidied up her sleeping bag and blankets in preparation for another night. It had been a rainy, chilly day and the family had spent the day inside. Occasionally the big dog came out into the yard, but even he was quick about his business and anxious to get back inside. The man had come out only briefly to let to gather wood from the porch. Emma could smell the smoke from a fireplace and though she wasn't curled up in front of it with people she loved, the smell alone helped warm her heart a little bit. She was quiet and careful whenever she needed to go out to use her makeshift "bathroom." She had cleared away some of the grass form a little spot behind some bushes where she was well hidden from the house. It wasn't really fun having to "go" outside, but Emma used her imagination to help make it easier. Sometimes she would pretend she was on a big outdoor adventure, or sometimes she would pretend she was a little girl back in pioneer days when they didn't have indoor bathrooms. Emma had loved watching old episodes of Little House on the Prairie and often imagined what it would have been like to be Laura Ingalls. With those thoughts on her mind, Emma pulled out her pencil once again and added toilet paper to her list of supplies.

When night again fell in earnest, Emma was both comforted and disturbed by the darkness. She knew she was safe from being found so she could relax about that, but the total darkness and silence made her more than a little bit lonely. She pulled on the warm sweater and curled up in her new sleeping bag, tucking the stuffed dog she always carried with her under her head for a pillow.

Inside the farmhouse, quite cozy in her new room, Brinn looked out over the dark meadow towards the big bulk of the old barn that stood outlined in the moonlight. "Maybe we'll get to explore that tomorrow if it stops raining," she whispered into Jasper's ear as she hugged him goodnight. Jasper licked her hand and did his usual round of spins before flopping down on his big foam bed.

Chapter 6

"Good morning sunshine," Sam said as he tousled Brinn's hair. "How was your first night in your new room? Sleep okay?

Brinn nodded her mouth full of the fresh apple muffins that Julia had just baked that morning. "I was a little scared of the dark at first, but Jasper slept right by my bed all night!"

"What big plans do you and Jasper have for today?" Sam asked as he finished pouring his coffee and brought it to the table, stopping to give Jasper a scratch on the way.

"We're going to explore some more, "replied Brinn with all of her usual enthusiasm. "Can me and Jasper look around in the old barn today?"

"Jasper and I," corrected Julia as she walked into the kitchen, and "I'm not sure if that would be a good idea. It's pretty run down and could be unsafe." Julia looked to Sam.

"I think it would be okay as long as you're really careful and promise not to be too much of a daredevil. Just have a look around but don't touch stuff or climb up those old stairs to the loft."

"I won't "promised Brinn with all her typical five year old confidence. "We'll be really careful. I just want to see what it's like inside. Come on, Jasper, let's get ready!" Brinn ran upstairs to get dressed and ready for another day of adventure, Jasper at her heels.

Out in the loft, another young girl was also getting ready to face the day. Emma had been out already to her little spot behind the barn. She had washed up a bit in the stream, but the water was getting really cold and it wasn't very much fun. She quickly ran back into the barn and up to the loft, pulling the blankets around her once again just to get warm. Just as she got settled, she heard the screen door of the porch slam, followed instantly by barking and the happy singing of the little girl. Cuddled in her blanket cocoon, Emma didn't move to the window to see what they were doing. She assumed the girl and dog would be hunting for rabbits or digging for vegetables or playing a game of fetch as they had done the day before. It wasn't until she heard the creak of the barn door that she realized they were coming into the barn. Emma froze. There was nothing she could do but stay as still as she could and hope they didn't climb the ladder to the loft.

Spooked a little by the dark dusty interior of the barn, Brinn wandered around the almost empty space whispering her thoughts to Jasper. "This place is kind of creepy," she said, keeping one hand on Jasper's scruff. She took in the big open space, the few old wooden crates stacked against one wall, and the rickety looking ladder that led to the loft. A concerned barn swallow that heard her come in swooped above her head before perching on one of the high rafters. Brinn gave a little screech at the sudden movement, and Jasper barked, making her jump again. When she realized it was nothing but a bird, Brinn laughed and plopped herself down on the bottom step of the ladder. "That was scary," she said out loud to Jasper, and then she laughed. "Some explorers we are, getting scared by a little bird!" Jasper barked in agreement.

Suddenly Jasper's nose went straight up in the air and he began taking big sniffs of the musty barn air. Next he started to bark and pace all around the bottom of the ladder. "It's ok, Jasper" Brinn reassured him. "It was just a bird." When Jasper refused to stop barking, Brinn's heart started to beat faster and she got a little scared. Jasper just kept barking and pacing and looking up into the loft. Brinn jumped up off the bottom step of the ladder and tried to get a look into the loft. From where she stood she could only see into a small portion of the loft, but as far as she could tell, the space was empty. There was no sound coming from the loft and Brinn wondered what Jasper was getting all excited about. He had stopped barking now, and stood resting his front paws on the bottom step where Brinn had been sitting. He was looking directly into the loft now, bushy tail wagging and his occasional short bark changing almost to a whimper from time to time. Brinn was curious to know what he might think was up there, but she was also a bit creeped out. In her five year old imagination, even as brave as she was, thoughts of monsters and creatures and scary things loomed larger than life.

"Come on, Jasper," she coaxed. "I think we've done enough exploring in here for one day." She grabbed Jasper's collar and tried to move him toward the door. At first Jasper stood unmoving near the bottom of the ladder. "Jasper, come on!" Brinn pleaded. "I want to go home, now." At the change in his master's tone, Jasper looked away from the ladder, and still with some hesitation, followed her to the door.

Up in the loft, Emma breathed a sigh of relief when she heard the barn door creak closed. She started to realize just how hard it was going to be to stay hidden, especially now that the dog knew she was there. With a feeling of despair, Emma realized that having this family move into the old farm house had given her a false sense of security, almost as if she'd be able to live her secret life here, unnoticed and happy, supported just by their proximity. She was suddenly very sad and very confused. Maybe it was time to move on. As Emma sat and pondered what her next move should be, a plan started to form in her mind. If she could get into town, maybe she could find a warm place to hide out and make a home for herself. She had watched TV shows where kids had lived in old churches or schools all by themselves, getting handouts from store owners and people on the street. Maybe she would even find other runaway kids there to hide out with. All she had to do was get into town. She knew that the man had a pickup truck that he often took into town. If she could sneak up to the house and hide in the back of the truck, then she should be able to get into town. From there, she would search for another hiding place. Emma decided that for now, the best thing for her to do was to stay quiet, stay hidden, and try to figure out when to make her big move.

It was hard keeping track of the days of the week when every day seemed the same, but she figured the man would probably go to his job most weekdays. Emma decided she would watch for a while and get to know his regular routine. It would have to be soon, though, because her supplies were running low and the old barn was getting pretty cold at night.

As the day wore on, Emma alternated between watching what was going on around the house, and writing notes in her little book. She was afraid to venture out as long as the family was home, so the day was long and boring. At some point after she had eaten the last of the food that she had, she drifted off into a restless sleep. When she awoke again, the sun was setting behind the house. The days seemed really short now, and soon she would face another long, lonely night.

Chapter 7

Emma watched the smoke from the chimney as it made a curling trail into the sky. How she longed to sit by the fire and soak up its warmth. She was starting to think that maybe leaving the Lindstrom's had been a bad idea, for as unhappy and lonely as she had been there, at least she was warm and well fed. She supposed another option would be for her to turn herself in to the family in the house and accept that she might be returned to the Lindstrom's or sent somewhere else if they no longer wanted her.

It was a very lonely feeling to be only ten years old and think that no one wanted you. Emma felt the tears well up in her eyes and slowly trickle down her cheek. Her hand was in mid air to wipe them away when she heard the barn door creak slowly open once again. She instinctively lowered her hand to her side and pulled herself silently into a small ball. She listened so hard for any sounds from below that she thought her ear drums would pop. She didn't hear any footsteps or voices, just the slight creaking of the door. Maybe the wind had just blown it open. She waited silently until she couldn't wait any longer, and then she crept to the edge of the ladder and peered down. Her eyes were met by another pair of equally brown, equally surprised eyes set into a wide furry face with a broad snout. Their eyes locked, and for what seemed like forever to Emma, neither dog or girl moved. Then the bushy tail began to wag and the black line on the dog's muzzle seemed to curve up in a smile. When Emma finally tore her eyes away, she glanced behind the dog for the person she was certain would be there, but no one appeared.

The dog now had his paws resting on the bottom rung of the ladder almost implying that, if she didn't come down soon, he was coming up. Emma stood to a low crouch and edged her way toward the ladder, taking a quick look through the crack in the barn wall to see what was going on at the house. There was no sign of anyone outside, and the doors were all closed. Emma could make out some movement in the kitchen through the lacey curtain, but the windows were closed to the chilly fall air and she couldn't hear any voices. When she glanced down the ladder again, she was met with the same brown eyed gaze as before.

Now there seemed to be a question there. "Why won't you come down and see me?" the furry mutt seemed to say. "I just want to be your friend!" Emma smiled in spite of herself and finally couldn't resist. With one last glance behind the dog, she lowered herself onto the first step of the ladder. The closer she got, the faster the dog's tail wagged and he began to prance in place, his nails clicking softly on the old wooden floor. Hoping with all her might that he wouldn't start barking, Emma jumped off the last step of the ladder and hugged the big scruffy neck. She buried her face in the wonderful woodsy smell of dog that she remembered from the old days. As if he understood her need for love, Jasper flopped to the floor and let this new little girl hug him just as he had allowed Brinn to do when they had first met. For Jasper, giving and receiving love was what made the world go round, with the odd game of fetch and a bowl of kibble thrown in for good measure. He stayed still until he felt her start to draw away.

"What are you doing out here all by yourself?" she asked. "And how did you get the door open?" Emma took another suspicious glance around as if asking the question would make someone appear. Maybe the little girl had left it unlatched earlier, she told herself, and this guy just happened to be out doing some necessary doggie business. If that was the case, someone would be calling for him soon, or even more likely, would come looking for him. Emma had to get the dog back outside and on his way home without getting herself discovered.

"Come on big guy," she whispered into Jasper's ear. "It's time for you to go home." She gave him one last hug and the pulled him towards the door by his collar. Stubborn as always, Jasper refused to budge. He knew this little girl needed his help, and she wasn't going to get it by his leaving her behind. Emma tugged and tugged on the collar but the dog was too heavy for her to move without his cooperation.

"Please go home now," Emma pleaded. "You can't stay here. Please go back home." Desperate to be safe again, Emma went to the back of the dog and tried to push him forward toward the door. Meeting only more resistance, Emma couldn't help but start to cry. "You have to go. Now." She whispered tearfully. Jasper sensed her emotional upset and turned to lick the tears from her cheeks. Emma was so taken back by this sudden show of compassion, that she came completely undone.

All of the loneliness, fear and uncertainty of the past few days released itself as she slid to the floor once again and sobbed into the the warm fur under her hands. She forgot to be careful. She forgot to be quiet. She forgot everything except how good it felt to let all her feelings go. Jasper sat uncomplaining in the same spot, determined to help his new little friend with the broken heart. Only when he heard his other young masters' voice calling from the back porch did he stand to contemplate leaving. Sensing his indecision, Emma quickly pushed him towards the door, before she herself headed up the ladder to the loft. Jasper glanced back at the girl one last time as if to say, "I'll be back, don't you worry." And then he turned and went out into the early evening. Emma waited until she heard the screen door to house slam shut before she scurried down and quickly latched the old barn door.

Early the next morning Emma was awakened by the sounds of the old pickup truck pulling out of the drive. Not more than a few minutes later, Emma watched from the cracked wall of the barn as the little girl and the dog left with the woman in the small green car. Excited that this could be her chance to get into the house once again, Emma hurried down the steps, creating a cloud of dust as she jumped from the third step to the floor. She paused only briefly to have a quick look around before she headed towards the house.

The view down the road was blocked by the house from this angle, so she didn't see the yellow truck until it was all the way up the driveway. Emma's heart started beating wildly as she ducked behind the small shed that had been built near the vegetable garden for housing tools and gardening supplies. She heard the doors of the truck slam and the loud voices of two men reached her clearly. They were walking straight to the old barn. The combination of cold and fear had Emma shivering from head to toe. She had fled the barn so quickly, not wanting to waste any time getting what she needed from the house that she hadn't bothered to put on the warm sweater or her jacket. Now the cold seemed to be going right to her bones. She hugged her arms around herself as she crouched low behind the shed. She had no trouble making out the conversation that the two men were having.

"Guess this must be the one," said the larger of the two men. "It's the only barn I see around here."

"Yep," replied the other man. "Let's get inside and have a look around."

Emma stayed as still as she could as she imagined the two men discovering her little hiding place and seeing all her belongings. What would they think? What would they do? Would they tell the man who lived in the house that someone was hiding in his barn? Should she run away now before they had a chance to find her? It took all the resolve Emma had to hold back the tears that threatened to flow. I have to be quiet. I have to be quiet. Emma repeated the words like a mantra over and over in her head.

Just when she thought her feet would fall off from being so cold, the two men emerged from the barn. It was the big man's voice again that she could hear. This time he was talking on a cell phone. He was telling someone that it was his recommendation that the old barn be torn down. There was nothing worth saving, in his opinion, and he could come back and finish the task in the next day or two. In the meantime he recommended that they cut down the old stairs to the loft right away as they could pose a real risk to anybody who might try to use them. Thinking of Brinn, Sam agreed to the demolition and to the immediate removal of the old ladder. The big man disconnected and filled his partner in on the plan. "We're going to cut down the old ladder to the loft today, and come back to finish the demolition of the whole barn, the day after tomorrow. I'll head back to the truck for the gear and you take a quick look around the loft in case there's anything we should move down.

Emma couldn't believe her ears. They were going to find her things and they were going to cut down the ladder! And there wasn't one single thing she could do, except stay where she was until they were done and gone. Once they were both back inside the barn, Emma crept around the corner of the little shed and slipped inside. It was at least a little bit warmer in there, out of the wind, but there was barely enough room for her to fit. She crouched down in the corner and waited while the buzz of the chain saw tore apart the only home she had.

Chapter 8

Brinn opened the car door and jumped out, eager as always to greet the day. She absolutely loved being a big girl and going to school every day. She was a good student and the teachers often commented on her quick ability to absorb information. There didn't appear to be any delays caused by the entire year that she was unable to speak. The psychologists and teachers all agreed that even though she hadn't been speaking, the normal range of learning had still been taking place. She now chattered as much as any other five year old, and maybe even more. As she scrambled to gather her things from the seat of the car, Julia reminded her that her father would be picking her up at the end of the day. "I'm going over to Wilmot to visit for a bit with Henry. There are some things around the farm that he left there, and we need to know if he wants some of them. I won't be back in time to get you but your Dad will be here."

"Are you taking Jasper with you?" Brinn asked.

"I am indeed," replied Julia. "Henry would never forgive me if I didn't!" Brinn laughed.

"Okay, Mom. Say hi to Henry for me. See you when you get home." Off she went, skipping her way to the door of the school. Julia waited until she was inside then drove away. Visiting hours at the hospital didn't start until one o'clock, so her plan was to spend the morning continuing with unpacking and organizing. She was anxious to get that part of the move over with so she could move on to decorating the nursery. Sam had already done the painting but he was leaving the decorating up to her. Her doctor had told her that there was a possibility that she could go into labor early, and with only six weeks left until her due date, Julia wanted to have everything ready in plenty of time to spend the last week or so relaxing and preparing for the ordeal that she had heard that labor could be.

As they pulled into the driveway Jasper started getting fidgety. He was ready to get out of the car and get on about his doggie business. He usually stuck pretty close to home on days when Brinn was at school, but today he seemed particularly anxious to go exploring. As soon as Julia opened the car door he was off and running. He stopped briefly along the edge of the drive to relieve himself, and then took off towards the old barn. He had his nose to the ground like a hound on the hunt. Julia smiled to herself. Sam had just texted her to say that the men had been to the house to inspect the old barn, and she was pretty sure that their scent was probably lingering around, giving Jasper good cause to be suspicious. She watched him for a few minutes until she was sure he wasn't going to go far, and then she headed on into the house.

Meanwhile, Jasper continued to sniff all around the perimeter of the barn. He could smell the men who had been there, but he could also smell the new acquaintance he had made the other day. He followed her scent to the little shed by the garden and then back again to the barn. He sensed that she was upset and in need of comfort. He started to whine softly in hopes that she might hear him and open the creaky old door so he could warm her with his furry coat and comfort her with some cold nosed kisses. Inside, Emma could hear the dog at the door. She was so distraught by what she had found when she returned to the barn, that she didn't even hesitate to let him in. She opened the door just a crack and Jasper slithered through the small opening. Emma sank to the dusty floor right there beside him and let her lonely tears fall on the soft fur. Starved for personal contact, she hugged him close and let all her feelings pour out. She told him all about the men who had been at the barn and how they had moved her things out of the loft and put them in an old crate. She sobbed as she told him that the old barn was going to be torn down, so that now, without a hiding place, she would have to leave right away or risk being found. "I don't know what to do," she cried into the floppy brown ears. "I just want a home, and a family and someone who wants me." As if he understood, Jasper started licking the tears from her cheeks. "I wish you could be my dog too," she whispered.

"Jasper!" The voice carried across the meadow and startled Emma. Instantly alert and focused, she stood and pushed Jasper towards the door. "Go, shoosh. Go home," she pleaded as she nudged him through the crack. "You can't stay here. Go!" Jasper, confused by her sudden change in mood, stood wavering with indecision, half in and half out of the doorway. "But I came here to help you," the big brown eyes seemed to say. "If I leave you now, you'll be sad again." But his new little friend seemed so intent on his leaving, that he finally gave in. With one last bright eyed look that seemed to say, "I'll be back," he was off and heading for the house where Julia was just coming out to find him. As he rounded the side of the barn, she stopped and waited for him to come to her. "And just where have you been, you little rascal? Doing a little exploring of your own are you?" She scratched the big brown head and let her hand rest on his back as they walked back to the house.

Inside the barn, Emma sank to the floor once again and tried to decide what to do. There wasn't any way she could leave the barn today. It was already mid afternoon, and the days were so short now she was worried that she would have to spend the night outside. She decided that she would wait until morning and then try to sneak into the back of the man's' truck. Once she was in town, she would have the day to find shelter, and hopefully some food. But for now, for tonight, she would have to stay here in the barn. She glanced around, hoping she could find some way to stay hidden just for this night.

The men who had cut down the stairs to the loft had put all her things in one of the old crates that were stacked in one corner of the barn. As Emma started removing them from the crate, she decided to use the pile of boxes to create her new hiding place. She pushed them together to form a little cubby where she could just barely fit to lie down. She spread out her sleeping bag and blankets along the wall and stuffed her backpack underneath to serve as a pillow for sleeping and for something to lean against during the day. She knew that anyone coming into the barn could easily find her, but she was at least a little bit hidden if they didn't venture all the way into the barn. By the time she had that little task completed, she heard voices coming from the direction of the house. No longer able to see the house from her viewpoint on the second level, Emma had to rely on her ears to tell her if someone was heading towards the barn. She squeezed herself into the new little space she had created and stayed perfectly still. The voices she could hear belonged to the man and the little girl. They sounded as though they were heading towards the barn and Emma's heart started to race. She heard the man say, "It's coming down tomorrow. It's way too dangerous to leave standing, and I can't risk having you or anyone else getting hurt. I just want to check and make sure the door is closed tight so Jasper doesn't decide to wander in here." They were just on the other side of the barn now, and Emma thought for sure her time was up. Her breath caught when she heard the old door hinges rattle. Closing her eyes tight and clenching her hands together she chanted "Please don't let them see me, please don't let them see me" She was so deep in concentration that she didn't realize at first that they hadn't even tried to get in, but merely ensured that the door was secure. Their voices were now growing faint as the girl and man walked back towards the house. Emma released her breath and relaxed her taut muscles. Tomorrow she would make her move. Tomorrow she would sneak into the truck and get away into town.

"Did you have a nice visit with Henry?" Brinn asked Jasper as he greeted her with back end wagging and pink tongue drooling. "I'll bet he was glad to see you!"

"He certainly was," Julia added. "I think it makes his whole day when we drop by." Turning to Sam, she added, "Henry says to dispose of anything we don't want. Wendy has already taken the things she wanted and has given Henry all of his personal things that he can keep with him."

"Good to know," nodded Sam. "Once we get that old barn torn down and all the junk hauled away, things will start looking a lot neater around here. The construction guys took the old stairs to the loft down today just for safety purposes, and they plan on being here first thing in the morning to get started on the demolition."

"We'll have to keep a close eye on Little Miss Curious here, and her furry sidekick," Julia said, nodding towards Brinn and Jasper. "If we don't, the two of them will be right underfoot!" They both laughed agreeably and watched as Brinn rolled a ball across the floor for Jasper.

Chapter 9

The next morning dawned crisp and clear. Emma was awake long before she heard any sounds coming from the house. She had already been out to her makeshift bathroom and was busily packing what she could into her backpack. She wanted to be sure that she made it to the truck before anybody woke up. She knew that once the big dog was let outside, he would make his way right back to her, and she couldn't let that happen. As she tucked her stuffed dog into the very last bit of space in her pack, she started to get butterflies in her stomach. It was scary to think of being out in the world all alone again. For the first time she truly realized how much comfort she had felt just being near this happy family, especially since the big scruffy dog had found her and become her friend. How good it had felt to hug him and snuggle up close. But Emma also knew that there was no place for her in this close knit group. They already had a little girl, and a dog, and when Emma saw the lady on the porch the other day, she realized that soon they would be having another baby too. There was no way they would want some runaway ten year old who was probably already on everybody's bad list by now. She was certain that getting caught now would likely mean being returned to the group home instead of foster care so she wouldn't cause any other poor foster parents a lot of trouble. Nope, her only solution now was to sneak into the truck, get into town and find a new place to hide.

With one last look around at the place that had been her home for the past several days, Emma threw her knapsack over her shoulder and headed for the door. Before she even had a chance to pull on the old rusty handle, the sounds of loud machinery reached her ears. What was that? Emma was afraid to open the door and check on where and what was going on, but she was even more afraid of hiding inside where she was almost certain to be seen by anyone coming into the barn. In a moment of panic, she pulled the old door open just wide enough to stick her head out to see what was going on.

Her panic grew as she watched a large machine with a giant bucket on the front heading towards the barn. Behind it, another smaller machine followed, like two monsters engaged in a game of follow the leader. Both were heading directly towards the barn. Following close behind the two machines, were the two men that Emma had seen the other day at the barn, and the man from the house. They were talking loudly to be heard over the noise sand gesturing towards the barn. Next in line, but some distance back, the lady from the house was walking with the little girl and the big dog. She was holding tight to the girl's hand, and the dog was on a leash. They stayed back as the machines and the men reached their final destination. Obviously, they wanted to watch what was going on, but the lady was going to keep them out of harms' way. Scared almost into paralysis, Emma ducked back into the barn and closed the door. Instinctively, she ran back into the little cubby she had made. Her heart was racing and tears were pouring down her face. She sank down onto the dirt floor hugging her knees and sobbing.

The machines were right outside the barn now but Emma could no longer hear any voices. She had no idea what was going to happen next. All she wanted was for it all to be over.

Satisfied that everything was being done safely, Sam told the men to go ahead and get started. He walked back to where Julia and Brinn were watching from a safe distance. With her great sense of adventure, there was no way Brinn was going miss taking in this event. Sam put his arms around her shoulders and held her close while Julia stood next to them with Jasper on his leash.

Just as the first machine reached the side of the barn, Jasper broke free and headed straight for the barn. His sudden movement took Julia completely by surprise and the leash slipped right through her fingers.

"Jasper, here!" both Sam and Julia yelled in unison. But the big furry dog was running frantically towards the big machine , barking as loud as he could. Julia and Sam stared in terror as he placed himself right in between the barn and the machine. The man in the driver's seat looked down in disbelief. Just one minute more, and the dog would have been crushed by the giant tracks of the machine. He idled the machine and leaned out the window. By this time, Sam was heading for the barn to retrieve Jasper. He grabbed the leash and tried to pull Jasper back and out of danger, but the big dog proved stronger than he expected. Jasper stood his ground barking, and whining in front of the barn door. Sam continued to pull on the leash, eventually losing patience and yelling for the dog to get going.

Frightened by her dad's anger, and Jasper's unusual behavior, Brinn began to cry. All of a sudden she was right there too, trying to hug Jasper and pleading with her dad to stop yelling at him. Both men were out of the machines now, just watching the weird turn of events, wondering if the dog had gone completely mad. Eventually, Sam was able to calm Brinn and grab the end of Jasper's leash. The crazed barking continued, however, mixed every so often with a long sad howl. Having gotten to know Jasper so well since his rescue, Julia sensed there was a lot more going on here than anyone knew. She walked up to Jasper and took the leash from Sam. At first Sam was reluctant to let go. "Julia, you could get hurt if he decides to go crazy again. Let me get him back to the house." But Julia just shook her head.

"I know it sounds crazy, but I think he's trying to tell us something. I really think he has a problem with us tearing down the barn. Maybe this has triggered some memory from his past, or maybe there is something inside the barn that he's trying to protect. I have no idea what it could be, but I think we owe it to him to at least take him in and have a look around."

"You better do something!" shouted the boss of the construction crew. "We're not getting anything done as long as that mutt's in the way. Time is money and you're wasting a lot of it trying to figure out what some dumb mutt is thinking!"

Sam glared at him. "Well, it's my money, so you just hang tight and don't worry about it. And as for Jasper being some "dumb mutt", you'd be smart not to let my wife or my little girl hear you say that. They wouldn't waste any time showing you just how smart he can be!"

Turning back to Brinn and Julia, he said calmly, "Ok, let's go see if we can find out just what Jasper is getting all worked up about!"

Emma sucked in a big breath and held back her tears when she heard the big old door creak slowly open.

Coming in out of the bright sunshine made it hard to see anything inside the dusty barn. Sam, Julia and Brinn stood just inside the door to let their eyes adjust to the darkness. Jasper didn't seem to suffer the same affliction, however, and he bolted across the open space and then stood barking. His masters followed him to a corner of the barn where several old crates were pushed together forming a little half wall. Jasper's bark turned to a whimper as they came closer.

"There must be something of Henry's in these old crates that he wants," Julia speculated. As she leaned over to peer into the top of the closest box, she sensed a very slight movement out of the corner of her eye. Thinking it might be a mouse or some other unfriendly barn creature, she jumped back. Grinning knowingly, Sam rounded the corner where there was a small opening in the group of boxes. He was prepared to watch a mouse scurry by, or even perhaps to chase a wandering raccoon back to the great outdoors. What he was not prepared for, was to see two big brown eyes looking back at him from under some very wild brown hair that fell in dirty strands around a tear streaked face. Before he even had a chance to speak, Jasper was pushing by him. The big old dog settled himself right beside the little girl and began licking away her tears. She smiled in spite of herself, and Sam looked on in wonder.

With one finger on his lips, he motioned silently for Julia to bring Brinn over. They huddled together, watching the dog and girl interact as though they had been friends forever. When Jasper at last looked up to see his people hovering nearby, he started running back and forth from one to the other as if making introductions. Mesmerized, Julia and Sam just stood there, but Brinn had no qualms about joining the party. She skipped right over to the spot where this new found friend still crouched in fear. "Hi," she said. "My name is Brinn, and this is my dog Jasper. I think he likes you. He can be your dog too, if you want!" The sad brown eyes drifted back and forth from adults, to dog, to the little girl, unable to make direct contact. Suddenly recognition dawned, and Julia came forward and knelt down beside the tiny figure. "You're Emma, aren't you?" she asked softly. "It's okay, you don't have to be afraid. No one here is going to hurt you."

Emma nodded and the tears began to flow once again. "Please don't send me back. I can't go back." She was sobbing now, and Jasper was almost beside himself. He paced frantically back and forth between Sam and Emma, stopping long enough each time to lick her face, hoping to provide comfort and stop her tears. Julia held out her hand to Emma, speaking gently the whole time. "Let's get you inside and warmed up, and then we'll talk, okay? And don't worry, we're not sending you anywhere." Brinn smiled at Emma and took her other hand as they walked out of the barn. Sam turned to Julia and nodded towards the house.

"You guys head on home, I'll see to the work out here." Before they had gone more than a few steps, Sam caught up with them to ask if Emma had anything else in the barn that she wanted. Emma raised her sad eyes to Sam's and shook her head. "Everything I brought with me is here in my bag," she said patting her backpack. Feeling his own eyes well up, Sam turned back towards the barn, while the others headed for the warmth of the house.

Brinn chattered away while they removed coats and boots and got Jasper settled down with a big chew bone. It was the only way they were going to stop him from licking the skin right off Emma's face. Julia led Emma into the big warm kitchen but didn't stop there. "I think a warm bath is the first thing on the agenda," she said as she led Emma up the stairs. "Then food, then talk, ok?" Emma had said very little up to this point but the lady and the little girl were so friendly that she finally relaxed a little bit.

"I haven't had a bath in a long time," she said quietly but with obvious longing.

"I know," said Julia, smiling. "And I think lots of smelly bubbles are called for too!" She filled the tub and watched Emma's eyes light up with anticipation. "You take just as long as you need, and here are some clean clothes for you to put on. They're from a bag of hand me downs that a friend gave me for Brinn . They may not be a perfect fit but they'll do for now." With that she closed the door and left Emma alone to enjoy the first pleasant thing that had happened to her in a long time.

Outside the hum and buzz of machinery told Julia that the barn demolition was back underway. She checked to make sure Jasper and Brinn were still safe and sound in the kitchen. She was amused to see Brinn sitting beside Jasper as her chewed away, telling him what a good dog he was for saving Emma.

"You are a real hero," she whispered into his ear. Brinn somehow felt that it was necessary to speak right into Jasper's ear when she had something important to say. That was exactly what she had done that very first time she spoke after a year of silence. Julia felt tears sting her eyes as she remembered that sweet sweet voice whispering "My doggie. My doggie for keeps," in Jasper's ear. Since that day, Brinn had chattered nonstop to her new loyal and loving friend. Brinn looked up, sensing Julia watching her, and smiled.

Julia bent down and gave her daughter a huge hug. "You are awesome," she said. "And so is your furry friend, there. You guys were great with Emma."

"Is she going to live with us?" Brinn asked expectantly as though it should be just that simple.

"I don't know what's going to happen, honey" Julia said. "We have to talk to Emma first and then figure out what to do."

"Well I hope she can live with us," Brinn insisted. "Then Jasper could be her dog too." Julia smiled and brushed the hair that had escaped from Brinn's ponytail out of her eyes, letting the conversation drop.

After a while Julia headed back upstairs and tapped on the bathroom door. "Everything okay in there?" she called. She was answered by the door opening and a fresh clean face smiling back at her. The straggly brown hair was clean and all traces of grit and grime were gone. Julia was amazed at the transformation. Standing in front of her was one of the cutest little girls she had ever seen. The big brown eyes were now sparkling and alert. Deep dimples appeared in each cheek when she smiled. Her upturned nose suggested just a bit of the determination and spunk that had probably helped her survive whatever tragedies life had obviously thrown her way. It took Julia a minute to find her voice. "Well don't you look good!" she finally said.

"The bath was awesome," Emma said. "Thanks."

"No thanks, necessary. Now let's get you downstairs and get some food into you." They walked silently together into the kitchen where Brinn and Jasper were still waiting. Brinn jumped up and ran over to Emma. Jasper was right on her heels and in that moment, Emma felt more welcome than she had in a very long time.

"Hi," she said simply, smiling at Brinn and giving Jasper a rub. They sat together at the table while Julia made a hearty breakfast of bacon, eggs, potatoes, toast and muffins.

Sam walked through the door just as they were about to sit down. "Smelled the bacon all the way out to the barn," he laughed as he pulled up a chair beside the girls. "Well now," he said. "Look at these pretty ladies at my kitchen table!" Brinn giggled, and Emma smiled, making eye contact with Sam for the very first time. He too, was taken aback by the girl's transformation. He looked at Julia with raised brows and she nodded, understanding exactly what he was thinking.

They ate in silence for a while, and then suddenly Emma spoke. Overwhelmed by their acceptance and patience, she just couldn't help herself. All the fear and worry and loneliness of the past few days came pouring out like a bucket overflowing. Working backwards through the tragic events of the past six years, she told them all about running away from the Lindstrom's, and the foster home before that. She told them what she could remember about her parents being in the accident, and their cabin, and Tucker and how all she thought she wanted was to get back home and live where she remembered being happy.

Although she was able to tell her story without crying, both Julia and Sam were struggling to keep control of their emotions. No strangers to traumatized children, they listened with genuine care and compassion. When Emma was finished, Brinn was first to break the silence.

"My Mom died too," she said with a matter of factness that seemed far beyond her years. "But now Julia is my Mom and we have Jasper and we live here in Jasper's old house and you can live here too if you want." Ever the optimist, Brinn summed it all up in one easy sentence. Emma couldn't help but laugh.

"I would love to live here, too," she said. "But I don't think it would be quite that easy!" She looked again to Sam and Julia. "Do I have to go back to the Lindstrom's? I really didn't like it there." Sam and Julia looked at each other for a long moment and then Sam spoke.

"We will have to call Family Services and let them know that you're here, and that you're okay. If you like, we'll also ask if you can stay with us for a few days."

"I'd like that a lot," Emma said quietly.

"Good, then all that's settled for now. I'll call a friend of mine who works for the county and find out where we go from here. For now, though, let's have a look at what's left of the old barn!" They all headed out to the back porch where they could see what was happening without getting in the way. There was already very little left of the original structure. A big pile of wood now filled the old foundation. In a while, two large dump trucks were to arrive and all the rubble would be hauled away. They watched the machines for a while longer, then Brinn asked if she and Emma could go up to the spare bedroom to play. Most of Brinn's toys had been parked there after the move until the family room could be organized. They were concentrating on getting the nursery finished first so the smell of paint would be long gone before the baby arrived. Julia told them to go ahead, but to stay out of the nursery where cans of paint were sitting on the floor between coats.

While the girls were busy playing upstairs, Sam made the call to his friend Declan Moore, a social worker who often came to the high school where Sam taught Phys Ed. Declan was great with troubled kids and Sam valued his professional opinion. He hoped that Declan would be able to help them keep Emma from being thrown right back into the system. He and Julia had immediately agreed it would be good for Emma if she could stay with them for a while until she was a little more stable emotionally.

After hearing the whole story, Declan agreed to talk to the people in charge and do his best to have Emma assigned to them as a temporary foster home. He explained that a visit from family services would likely come first, which would also include separate interviews with each family member as well as Emma herself. A report would then be filed and a meeting held to approve the placement. If all of that went well, Emma would be theirs until a new, long term foster home could be found. He told them not to worry, that it all seemed pretty cut and dried, and that the ruling should go in their favor. Sam thanked him for his help and went to tell Julia what to expect. They decided not to say anything to Emma until they had received at least a preliminary response from family services.

Emma, Brinn and Jasper stuck together like glue for the rest of the day. Emma was super patient and accommodating with Brinn's request to play Candy Land for the fourth time. Then they went out and threw a stick for Jasper until he collapsed on the porch, his sides heaving and his huge pink tongue dripping enormous puddles of drool. Julia brought chocolate milk and cookies out to the porch while they rested in the late afternoon sunshine. Julia's heart warmed at the sounds of their chatter, and a gentle little flutter in her belly told her that someone else was also enjoying the sound. The baby was becoming more and more active, and Julia couldn't wait for him or her to be with them. What a family they would be!

As the sun settled behind the trees, Julia called to the girls to come inside. Sam built a fire in the living room and girls and dog stretched out to soak up its warmth. Emma, exhausted from the events of the day, dozed off with her head resting on Jasper's back, while Brinn pretended to read one of her favorite books to her captive furry audience.

Chapter 10

The call came from family services early the following morning. A pleasant young lady by the name of Susan, asked if she might pay a visit to them that afternoon. She explained that, since Emma had been on the run for some time, it was important that they see her soon to confirm her health and well being. Sam told her that she was fine, but also that he understood their concern and that they were welcome to come to the farm any time. An appointment was set for 3 in the afternoon of that day.

Emma paced around the house, unable to relax after Sam told her about the pending visit. He tried to reassure her that they were only coming to make sure that she was okay, and that they weren't going to take her away.

"My friend has put in a good word for us", he told a worried Emma. "You're going to be able to stay here for a little while at least." With those words of encouragement, Emma seemed to relax a bit.

'Thanks," she said simply. "I really like it here."

Sam smiled and gave her a hug. "And we like having you here."

In spite of their best intentions, by 3 o'clock everyone was on pins and needles. Jasper had once again been confined to the mud room with another chew bone, and Emma and Brinn sat playing cards quietly in the living room, without any of their previous joking and bantering. Sam paced the floor, although he had no idea why, while Julia tried to remain calm. The sound of the doorbell made them all jump and Jasper gave a half hearted bark, not wanting to interrupt his meal. Sam opened the door and introduced himself and the others. Susan Kellerman was friendly and professional as she spoke to Emma, obviously assessing her emotional and physical condition as they carried on a light conversation. With introductions and formalities out of the way, Susan asked if she could speak with Emma privately for a bit. Sam, Julia and Brinn left them alone and went to sit at the kitchen table. In just a few minutes, Susan poked her head into the kitchen and asked if she could now speak with Sam and Julia. Brinn was sent back to the living room to join Emma.

"Well," Susan began. "I must say, that is some brave little girl. She has been through a lot and yet she seems perfectly calm and collected right now. I think we owe a lot of that to you guys. I understand you'd like to apply for temporary placement?"

A look passed between Sam and Julia of total understanding. Julia nodded and Sam did the talking. "Actually," he said, maintaining eye contact with Julia as he spoke. "We'd like to apply to be Emma's long term placement." When Julia smiled, he turned his eyes to Susan.

Susan looked from Sam to Julia and smiled. "I see," she said. "I think that you would be fine candidates for foster parents. I'll file my report with my highest recommendations, and we'll see what happens! We should have an answer with the week. In the meantime, I can see that Emma is in the best of care." She rose and extended a hand to first Julia and then Sam. "Thank you. It was a pleasure meeting you. I'll just pop back into the living room and say goodbye to Emma. I'll let you folks fill her in on what's happening."

Sam and Julia decided only to tell Emma that she would be staying with them for a while. They didn't want to mention the application for permanent placement in case it didn't work out. They told her not to worry, and that they would do their very best to make sure that she was happy. Emma was accepting of the news, happy that she would be staying here for a little while at least. She was tired of hiding, tired of being alone, tired of having no one to love her. If these few days were all the happiness she would have, then she was going to enjoy them. She hugged each of them in turn, saving the biggest hug of all for Jasper. Like Brinn, she bent down and whispered right into his floppy ear. "Thanks for finding me, Jasper, and thanks for bringing me home. At least for a while, you can be my dog too." Jasper responded with a big wet kiss right on her cheek. Everyone laughed and headed back to their places by the fire.

Chapter 11

In the days that followed, the new little family grew even closer. Emma relaxed and her wonderful personality was permitted to shine through. Brinn blossomed even more with the attention of an instant older sister, and Julia and Sam enjoyed every minute with their "girls." They joked often that the baby better be a boy so that Sam wasn't so outnumbered, but it was all in good fun. Boy or girl, their only real wish was for a safe delivery and a healthy baby. Sam continued with the nursery and the girls went shopping together for baby clothes and accessories. Being busy made the time pass faster and Emma, especially was glad for that. As happy and relaxed as she was with Sam and Julia, the anxiety about finding a new foster placement was always there. She realized she was holding her breath every time the phone rang.

When the weekend rolled around with still no word, Julia suggested that Sam take the girls into town for lunch and a movie. Julia wanted to finish up some final paperwork before she went on maternity leave and needed some peace and quiet to get it done quickly. Sam agreed, and the girls were delighted. They ran upstairs to get ready with Jasper right on their heels. He didn't know what was going on, but he knew it must be good. The unfortunate thing he hadn't yet realized, was that he was likely going to be left at home. Waiting in the truck for more than three hours was hard on his joints now that he was getting older. He was always stiff after such trips, especially when the weather was cold. And besides, Sam really liked knowing that Jasper was home with Julia whenever she was there alone. Truth be told, the feeling was quite mutual. Julia liked the comfort and security of his big furry presence. Not that there was any need for a watchdog, or protector, but it was just nice to know he was there.

Now, with the girls and Sam gone, Julia found the house almost too quiet. She did have work that she wanted to get done, but the sound of Jasper snoring blissfully at her feet made her start to feel drowsy too. Instead of heading for the office, she sank down into the comfy living room sofa, drawing her knees up under her and resting her head on one of the overstuffed cushions. Before long she had drifted off. She was deep in a dream about summer time at the beach, where warm water was lapping around her feet and the sun was warm on her face.

Suddenly Jasper's incessant barking startled her awake. She opened her eyes slowly, and realized that maybe the part of the dream about water had come from the puddle of water that had soaked her right through as she slept. A searing pain across her mid section brought her fully awake and aware of what was happening. When the pain subsided, she shuffled to the kitchen to find her cell phone. Jasper stayed right by her side, whimpering now, satisfied that his barking had raised the necessary alarms.

Julia hit Sam's number on speed dial and prayed that he hadn't yet turned his phone off for the show. Thankfully, he answered on the second ring. "Hi, what's up? Miss us already?"

"I sure do," said Julia. "And if you don't turn around and come home right now, Jasper may need to deliver this baby!"

There was a second of silence and then a shout. "We're on our way. Should I call the doctor? Are you sure you're ok? Should we call an ambulance?"

"I'm fine. My water broke and I think contractions are starting. They aren't serious yet, so we should be okay. Just hurry, Ok? But drive safe."

"Be there in fifteen," Sam said abruptly and disconnected. He flipped the phone closed and rejoined the girls who had gone ahead to get in line to buy their tickets. "Show's gonna have to wait, ladies" he grinned. "Looks like we're having a baby today!"

Brinn jumped up and down, clapping her hands and grinning from ear to ear. Emma turned a worried face to Sam? "Isn't it too early?"

"It is, but Dr. Jameson said there was good chance Julia would deliver early. It's complicated to explain, but nothing we weren't prepared for. And nothing for you to worry about. Now let's get home!"

Jasper was right at the door to greet them when they got home. He jumped in circles, barking and whining, as much as to say, "I've done all I can. You take it from here." He led the way into the living room where Julia sat nervously waiting. She had changed her clothes and gathered up her hospital bag. Heddi James, an old friend from town was going to come over and stay with the girls while Sam was at the hospital. Julia turned to Emma and took both the girls hands in hers.

"Do you think you can take care of Brinn and Jasper until Heddi gets here? It shouldn't be too long." Emma pulled herself up tall and stuck out the determined chin that had seen her through much more difficult challenges than this.

"I sure can. Don't you worry, we'll be just fine." She said proudly.

"I know you will," Julia said and gave her hands a squeeze. She and Sam headed off to attend the next big event in their lives. "We'll call you as soon as there is any news." She called from the car as they pulled away.

Heddi arrived at the door not a half hour later. She was a pleasant grandmotherly sort who started fussing over them right away. Brinn and Emma decided that since they had missed the movies that afternoon, that they would watch one of the movies from Brinn's collection. Heddi agreed to make them some popcorn and hot chocolate. She said that was her granddaughter's favorite movie snack, so Emma and Brinn didn't argue. Things in the movie were just getting interesting when the phone rang. Thinking it was going to be news of the baby, they both jumped up and raced for the phone. Emma stopped short of picking it up, however, realizing with a jolt that it wasn't her place. This was Brinn's home, Brinn's family, and it was Brinn's new baby brother or sister who was arriving. Brinn sensed Emma's hesitation and understood. As much as she wanted to be the first one to hear the news, she motioned to Emma to pick up the phone, and was rewarded with the biggest grin she had ever seen on Emma's face. Emma picked up the handset and held it off to the side of her ear so Brinn could lean in and listen too. "Hello?" Emma said, expecting to hear Sam's voice. Instead, the soft voice of Susan Kellerman answered on the other end.

"Hello, is this Emma?"

"Yes, speaking," said Emma slowly. Her heart started pounding while she waited for the woman to say more.

"Is Julia or Sam there?" she asked.

"No. They're at the hospital. Julia is having the baby." Emma's voice now showed none of the excitement or anticipation that she had been feeling just two minutes ago. Suddenly she was scared, and all she could think about was not being a part of this family any more.

"Oh, I see, " said Susan. "Well, I guess it's a night for good news all around, then. I'm calling to let you know that Sam and Julia have been approved as your permanent foster placement. You'll be living with them from now on. I hope this makes you happy, Emma."

For a few minutes Emma couldn't speak. Then tears began to flow down her cheeks even though she was grinning that great big grin again. Finally, she realized Susan was still waiting on the line.

"Thank you. Thank you," was all she could think to say. Through the phone she could hear Susan laughing softly.

"You're welcome, Emma. Can you please ask Sam to call me when he has a moment? There's no big rush. We have paperwork to fill out, but it can wait. Tell him congratulations too okay?"

"I will," said Emma hanging up the phone. She and Brinn hugged and danced in circles, chanting and laughing and crying all at the same time. Jasper ran around them equally caught up in the excitement. They were making so much noise that they almost didn't hear the phone when it rang a second time. This time they picked it up together and leaned in to get the news they had been waiting for.

"It's a girl!" Sam's voice bellowed. "You have a new baby sister!"

"It's a girl," the girls relayed to an already teary eyed Heddi. "We've got a new baby sister." They listened while Sam gave them some details about the baby's weight and hair, and Julia's health. Then Brinn took the phone into her own hands and spoke directly into the mouthpiece.

"Dad, " she said seriously. "Emma has some good news too." She then passed the phone to Emma. Emma tried not to cry as she explained to Sam about the call from Susan Kellerman. She could hear the tears in Sam's voice when he told her how happy he was, and how happy Julia would be. He said he would be home as soon as Julia and the baby were settled for the night. "Good night, girls," he said. I'll be home soon."

The movie was abandoned as the two new sisters chattered about future plans for themselves and their new baby sister. They both hugged Jasper , who was by now completely exhausted by the day's events.

"Guess what, Jasper," said Brinn in a singsong voice. "You get to be Emma's dog and the new baby's dog too!"

Emma hugged Jasper even tighter. "Now you're my dog too," she whispered right into his ear. Jasper looked from one to the other knowing that something good was going on. His girls were happy, he was home, and all was right with the world.

The End

Cooper's Gift

DANA LANDERS

Cooper's Gift

Chapter 1

Heddi James had always loved Christmas. But this year she was dreading its arrival. This would be her first Christmas without Charlie. Her first Christmas without Cooper. Her first Christmas alone. Heddi wished she could just close her eyes and wake up in the new year, with all the festivities over. It had been a long, difficult year and she was tired. How could she even consider decorating and baking and shopping for gifts when she was still struggling with simple decisions like what to do with Charlie's things? It had only been six months since Charlie had suffered a major stroke and died at home in his sleep. As difficult and as sudden as his passing had been, Heddi was so grateful that Charlie had gone quietly at home without suffering. That would have been his choice, Heddi reassured herself time and time again. But with the holidays drawing near, she was feeling pressured to put away Charlie's things and get her life organized. There would be lots of company coming this year and it didn't seem right to have Charlie's things still as they had always been.

She was packing up a box of Charlie's fishing gear, hoping that perhaps one of the boys would like to have it. As she placed the last package of shiny colorful lures into the box, she could almost hear Charlie telling one of his fish stories. He had never had much success at this hobby which he had taken up so late in life, but he had taken all the teasing in good spirits. "That's why they call it fishing, and not catching!" he would say whenever one of the little ones asked him why he never caught anything. But he had sure enjoyed trying. Heddi suddenly felt the tears well up. "If only he'd had a little more time," she thought. But time hadn't been on Charlie's side. He had been snatched from her unexpectedly long before they had had time to do the things they planned. Now there would be no lazy days of retirement, no travels around the country, no Alaskan cruise. The loss was still so new that all Heddi had to do was think about Charlie and she would start to cry. She honestly didn't know how she was ever going to make it through Christmas.

But Heddi knew better than to dwell on her sorrow. Better to get back to the tasks at hand and keep busy. She wiped her eyes, straightened her shoulders and tucked in the corners of the box. She'd be sure to ask the boys about it next time she saw them.

"Naaaanaa!" Heddi heard the call, followed by the slamming of the screen door and she knew a sunny little face was about to appear. Her oldest daughter Kristen and her husband Dave lived in a big rambling century home right in the heart of the village. They had both grown up in Lilac Creek and had begun dating in high school. Nearly twenty years and three kids later, they were still the high school sweethearts they had always been. Missy, who just turned four, was their youngest. Devon and Blake were just over a year apart at eight and nine. Since Heddi lived just on the outskirts of town, the kids were close enough to walk over for a visit if they wanted to and Heddi encouraged them to drop by whenever they chose. She always enjoyed their company, even more so now that she was on her own. The boys were getting too old now for hugs and such, but they still loved to come over and chat about school or sports, and to sneak a few extra after school snacks before heading home. Missy still thought her Nana was "the best" because Heddi let her do all kinds of crafts like painting and pasting, and also let her help in the kitchen. They were great pals and Missy spent as much of her "off school" days as she could with her Nana. She was just as at home in Nana's house as she was her own, and Heddi liked it that way. So it never came as a big surprise to hear the slam of the screen door announce her arrival.

"Nana, where are you?" Impatient as always, Missy flew into the house looking for her.

"I'm in here," Heddi called from the TV room. "What's all the excitement about?"

'**We** are decorating this morning. Want to come and help? Mommy said we should do the outside before too much snow comes. She said we should come and get you because you love to decorate, and you were usually the first one to do any decorating and you haven't even started yet, so maybe it would help you find your Christmas spirit if you did something Christmassy, like helping us do ours!" She took a big breath, and with her hands on her hips, gave Heddi her best four year old "all business" look.

Heddi smiled and tousled the blond curls that were bobbing around as Missy talked. "Well, I would like to come help, but I really should keep at my chores."

Missy waved her hands emphatically. "But Nana," she said in that know it all tone that only little girls can get away with. "Doing chores is making you sad. Mommy said we have to try and make you get happy again. Helping us decorate will make you happy."

Heddi smiled in spite of herself. "Ok, Missy. Then I guess we'd better get going and do what Mommy says." As they turned to leave the room, Missy suddenly noticed the things that Heddi had been sorting, and her smile disappeared. She picked up one of her Papa's hats that had been put in the pile and touched it fondly. "I miss Papa," she stated sadly. "And I miss Cooper too." Heddi's heart ached for her. To suffer two such significant losses in so short a time had been really tough. Cooper, their 14 year old yellow lab, had passed away about three months before Charlie, and the loss had been especially hard on Missy who was an animal lover through and through. Unlike Charlie, Cooper's passing had not been sudden or unexpected. At 14, he had been suffering for some time with blindness, loss of hearing and advanced arthritis. Heddi and Charlie knew that his quality of life was slipping away and that very soon, Cooper would let them know that his time had come. Though the children could also see the difficulties Cooper was having, they didn't really understand what it would ultimately mean. When the time came, she and Charlie had called all the children together to say their goodbyes to the loyal friend that they had loved for their entire lives. It was especially hard to explain that what they were about to do was the best thing to do for Cooper. As each of the kids hugged his neck and stroked his silky coat, Cooper sat patiently, giving each one a soft lick in return, as his way of saying goodbye. Charlie had been the one to really help Missy cope with the loss. Cooper had been his dog and Missy was his little sidekick. The three of them spent lots of time together, and Missy still missed that connection.

Heddi knelt down and drew the little girl into her arms. "I know, sweetie. I miss them too. But we have Papa and Cooper right here in our hearts forever, right?"

"Right," Missy said, all chipper once again. "Papa didn't use to like it when I was sad, so I better not be sad." Heddi hugged her and marveled at the simple childlike logic.

"Now we better get going before Mommy has to come looking for us." Heddi grabbed her coat and pulled on her boots while Missy ran ahead to tell her Mommy that they were coming.

Chapter 2

Back at home later that evening, Heddi sat quietly reflecting on the day. She was tired, but it was a good tired. She had enjoyed the day outdoors with her daughter Kristen and the kids. Everyone had helped out with the decorating and the house looked fantastic. The two huge evergreens that flanked the house were adorned with several strings of white lights and more tiny twinkling lights sparkled among the lilac bushes that lined the lane. Each of the six windows in the front of the house glowed softly with a single white candlestick light. Kristen liked to keep the decorations simple and classic, but the kids wanted something a little more colorful so a huge inflated snow globe with a cozy Christmas scene inside stood large and bright in the rear yard where the kids could see it from the playroom.

Naturally, as soon as the decorating was done, Missy was on to the next thing. She wanted to know when they would be decorating Nana's house. Heddi tried to hedge about getting at her own decorating, however, by saying that she still had to pull everything out of the storage room. What she didn't say was that it used to be Charlie's job to get things out, and she was having some trouble accepting the fact that from now on it would be up to her. Heddi knew that her kids and grandkids were only concerned for her happiness, but these obstacles she was facing were going to have to be overcome in their own good time and in her own way. Somehow they just couldn't be rushed and try as she might, Heddi just couldn't find the motivation to do all the Christmas things alone that she used to do with Charlie and Cooper. A picture suddenly popped into her head of Cooper, leaping belly deep through the freshly fallen snow, while she and Charlie tried to find the perfect Christmas tree to cut down. As far as Cooper was concerned, the longer it took them to decide, the better because it meant more play time for him. Like Charlie, Cooper loved winter and being out in the cold and snow together was one of their favorite activities. They spent many a winter afternoon snow shoeing through the woods, enjoying all the beauty that only a winter wonderland in the north can provide. Then they would arrive home chilled to the bone and both ready for a nap by the fire.

As Heddi thought back on those days, she felt the happiness of the morning slowly slipping away. She wondered if she would ever be truly happy again. Deciding that maybe it was just all the expectations surrounding Christmas that had her feeling more down than normal, she decided to just relax with one of her favorite TV shows and not think about anything for a while. She brewed a good strong pot of tea and made a sandwich to take and eat in front of the TV. About halfway through the show, when returning her dishes to the kitchen, Heddi was surprised to see that her porch light had come on. It was on a motion sensor, which meant that someone or something was on her porch. She glanced at her watch. It was only six thirty, but complete darkness had fallen. Realizing that it was still so early, Heddi expected to hear a knock at the door, announcing the arrival of one of the kids, a salesperson, or a neighbor dropping by to say hello.

As she came into the living room, she could see out onto the porch through the front door window, and could tell there was no one standing there. "Must be that darn cat again," Heddi thought to herself. For a few nights now she had seen the old tom run off when she came to see what made the light come on. She supposed all the cats in the neighborhood felt a lot braver about coming around now that Cooper was gone, but they weren't visitors that she wanted to encourage. Heddi opened the door ready to shoosh the cat away, but to her surprise there was nothing there. She had a good look around but didn't see any signs of movement. Deciding that the cat had already run off or that it had been some other kind of wildlife, Heddi closed the door and headed back for the TV room. She was only a few steps from the door when she saw the light come on once again. "Oh, for heaven's sake," mumbled Heddi. Wondering what was going on, she headed for the front door once again and pulled it open. Her heart flip flopped in her chest as she saw movement out of the corner of her eye. She was certain that she had just seen a yellow lab like Cooper running off down her drive and into the woods. For just a second, thoughts of Cooper flashed through her mind, and then reality came back. She knew it couldn't have been Cooper, but had there been some other dog on the porch? Or was her mind just playing tricks on her? Maybe she was seeing things! Maybe she was even more stressed than she realized! But then, as Heddi stepped out onto the verandah, the porch light shone down on a small pile of dark objects right beside the door. She knelt down for a closer look and was surprised to see several large pine cones sitting there.

"What in the world are these doing here? And where did they come from?" Heddi gathered up the pine cones and carried them inside. She put them into the big bowl that sat on her hall table and pondered their arrival. As she looked them over, Heddi couldn't help but marvel at the size and the quality of the pine cones.

"They look just like the ones Charlie and I searched for every Christmas to decorated the verandah." Every year they would make an afternoon trek out into the woods, bundled up against the weather and wearing backpacks that contained a thermos of hot chocolate, ham and cheese biscuits and peanut butter cookies. Cooper looked forward to this day more than any other of the season, even more than finding and cutting the tree because they generally spent the entire day in the woods. He could run to his heart's content chasing squirrels, chipmunks and even the occasional rabbit. He also enjoyed the biscuits and cookies. Once their extra knapsacks were full of large, fragrant pine cones, they would head towards home cutting pine boughs as they went. Just the smell of the fresh cut pine, dampened by the wet snow, could always put Heddi in a happy Christmas mood. They would deposit all their treasures on the front verandah for safe keeping until the next day when the verandah would be transformed into a magical holiday display.

Heddi suddenly saw the dampness on the bowl of pinecones. She hadn't even realized she was crying.

"Oh, Charlie," she sighed. "How am I going to get through this? You were always my rock in times of trouble. You could give me a hug and make everything ok. So what do I do now?"

Heddi placed the pine cone back in the basket and sunk heavily into her favorite chair. She wasn't sure if she even wanted to decorate the verandah, and she was absolutely certain that she didn't want to go hiking in the woods by herself to find the pinecones and pine boughs. For a while she entertained the idea of doing something else with the porch, something simpler and easier for her to do instead. But doing something different seemed disloyal somehow. After all, one of her favorite sayings was "you don't mess with tradition." She used to tell Charlie that every holiday when he wanted to cook something different than the traditional dinner fare.

Thoughts of holiday traditions and unusual objects appearing on her porch out of nowhere were still on her mind as she dozed off, head back and feet up in her favorite chair.

Chapter 3

Sunday morning dawned sunny and cold with no forecast of snow. There was no place more beautiful than Lilac Creek in the winter, especially at Christmas time. As beautiful as it was in the spring, nothing could surpass the winter wonderland it became after the first snowfall. The shops in town were all decorated for the season, and you'd be hard pressed to find a house without some type of outdoor decoration. Since it was mostly a rural community, homeowners were eager to put up Christmas decorations that added a bit of light to their usually dark property. Heddi always loved their drives around the area to look at everyone's lights. She and Charlie would always vote for the house they thought had the best decorations, and leave a pretty holiday card in their mailbox thanking them for taking the time to share their holiday spirit with everyone.

Even though their cottage sat at the end of a really long drive, and was not visible to passersby, she and Charlie had always decorated it just the same. The verandah was always decorated with fresh pine boughs, swags of pine cones tied with bright red ribbon, and twinkling white lights. They had chosen this over putting lights on the roof so Charlie could avoid climbing up ladders and dealing with an icy rooftop. It sometimes seemed like a lot of effort, but it was a traditional they never passed on. They themselves enjoyed being welcomed home by the twinkling lights, and the grandkids loved seeing them whenever they came by. Heddi also felt warmed by the glow of the outdoor lights when she let Cooper out for his bedtime rituals.

Today, Heddi was glad to see the sunshine, and for a few minutes she considered getting all bundled up for a hike in the woods. But just the thought of being out there alone, without Charlie, and without Cooper, depressed her. Maybe she just wasn't ready yet. Instead, she poured a second cup of coffee and settled down in her chair by the window where she could feel the sun on her face.

Sundays had once been their favorite day, but Heddi now found it to be the longest day of the week. Saturday she did her shopping and errands so that kept her busy for most of the day. During the week, she had babysitting obligations on the days that her daughters worked, and she was always ready to just go home and crash after a day with the grandkids. But Sundays were hard. Her daughters and their families were usually busy doing their own family things, and as lonely as she sometimes was, she didn't for a second begrudge them their time together. Both of her sons in law worked very long hours during the week and looked forward to their Sundays at home. Heddi and Charlie had never started a tradition of Sunday dinners with the family for just that reason. Instead, they had made Sunday their own special day for doing things together. Almost every Sunday morning without fail, they would hike the short trail that looped through the woods and then come back and make a hearty breakfast and a second pot of coffee to enjoy together. Heddi suddenly realized that she had not hiked the short trail once since Charlie had passed away. She and Charlie had continued to hike the trail after they lost Cooper, but it was never quite the same. Charlie had insisted that they go every Sunday anyway, just to honor Cooper's memory. She supposed she should be doing the same to honor both Cooper and Charlie, but Heddi just couldn't make herself go. Instead, she eventually pulled herself up from her chair and headed into the TV room once again to finish the sorting and packing that she had started the day before.

This time she completed the task and arranged three piles of boxes. She put one pile beside the front door to take to the donation center. The second pile she put off to the side. Each one of these boxes was marked with the name of the person who was going to receive those items. Their son Geoffrey was an avid reader and history buff so Heddi had packaged up some of Charlie's books for him. Heddi had decided to give much of Charlie's fishing stuff to Kristen and her family. They all loved to fish and had done so often with Charlie, so it only seemed fitting that they receive those things. Finally, Heddi had assigned some of Charlie's tools to her youngest daughter, Jenna and her family. She couldn't help but smile as she thought back onto many a home renovation that Charlie and Jenna had undertaken. They were birds of a feather, those two, and both had definite ideas on how to do things. Although this caused a fair number of eruptions during the course of the project, they always seemed to work things out and finish up doing a fantastic job when all was said and done. Heddi knew that Jenna would think of her Dad any time she used one of those tools, and that thought pleased her. The final pile of boxes contained sentimental items of Charlie's that Heddi wanted to keep but didn't necessarily want sitting about the house. They were things that she couldn't part with, but just wanted to save. She hoped there would come a day when she could take them out of the box and enjoy them and the memories that they held. But for now, Heddi would tuck them away in the storage room for safe keeping. As she headed towards the storage room to do just that, Heddi remembered that she had promised Missy that she would get her Christmas things out of storage so that they could decorate together the following week. She hesitated, hand on the door knob, trying to decide if she would get those out today or not.

She was saved from making that decision by a knock at the door. As she came out into the living room, her daughter Jenna walked in, followed by her husband Drew carrying what looked like a bundle of wiggling baby, various blankets and an assortment of brightly colored toys all linked together. Sammy, short for Samantha, was almost six months old and the happiest baby Heddi had ever seen. She was always smiling and gurgling. They had stopped by to invite Heddi to come out for dinner with them. Since Heddi had not really planned anything for her dinner, she was pleased to tag along. They visited for a few minutes then Heddi went to freshen up while Jenna changed and dressed Sam. Before long they were heading out the door to the local family restaurant. Heddi was grateful for the happy interruption of her packing and sorting. They enjoyed a great dinner with plenty of friendly chatter about this and that. Heddi told them about the unusual incident of her light coming on several times the night before for no obvious reason. She also mentioned the pile of pinecones that seemed to appear out of nowhere. Jenna laughed and said that maybe some crazy squirrel with an overactive Christmas spirit was trying to help her with the decorating. Drew told her she should be cautious because coyotes had been spotted hanging around his current work site which was not far from her house. Heddi just shrugged the strange occurrence off and promised that she would be careful if it continued to happen.

As usual, Sammy was content to watch the bright lights and all the people bustling by, but when she had decided those things were no longer so entertaining, she let them know it was time to get moving. Drew paid the bill while Jenna dressed Sammy and then they all headed back out into the cold evening. Darkness had fallen while they were inside and a light snow was beginning to fall, reminding Heddi once again that Christmas was steadily moving closer.

"So, when are you going to do your decorating, Mom?" Jenna asked. "You've usually got it all done by now."

"I know," Heddi replied. "Guess I'm just getting slow in my old age! I'm going to try and get at it this week. Missy has already been on my case and you know how insistent she can be!" Heddi made an attempt to sound light hearted about the whole thing but Jenna sensed the underlying hesitation.

"If it's too hard for you to do by yourself, we can do it together, you know," Jenna offered. Heddi wondered if she meant hard as in physically hard, or if she meant it in the emotional sense. Either way, Heddi thanked her for the offer and agreed that it would probably be a good idea to work at it together. She almost wanted to say that she would just as soon not do it at all, but she felt selfish for her thoughts. The kids had all had to deal with the loss of their father and it hadn't been easy for them either. But they also all had little ones to focus on, to keep happy, and to take their minds off of their loss. Heddi just felt so lonely and alone.

Sammy fell asleep on the drive home so Drew dropped Heddi at her door. They said their goodbyes from the warmth of the car and Heddi promised to call Jenna the next day to make plans for decorating. Heddi waved as they drove away and headed quickly inside to the welcome warmth of her cozy cottage. She was so grateful that Julia Henderson had helped her and Charlie find this gorgeous stone cottage a few years back when they decided to downsize from the family home to something more manageable. Julia had worked tirelessly to find them just what they were looking for. Heddi didn't see Julia all that often, but she knew that Julia had recently married Sam Baxter, the high school gym teacher, and that their little girl Brinn was thriving. Heddi and Julia had met up several times at the dog park where she used to take Cooper. Julia and Brinn would often be there with Jasper, and both the dogs and their owners always had a great visit. Heddi reflected back on those dog park days as she carried a cup of tea to her favorite chair.

She was no more than nicely settled in when her porch light came on once again. "Well for the love of Pete," Heddi mumbled, sounding just like Charlie. She pulled herself out of her chair and shuffled in her fuzzy slippers to the door. Thinking about what Drew had said about coyotes, she peered through the window first before opening the door. When she didn't see anything on the porch or in the yard, Heddi opened the inside door and looked around for a bit while keeping the storm door closed. When she still saw no signs of movement, Heddi opened the screen door and stepped out onto the porch. There was no sign of any living thing, and Heddi even looked around on the porch expecting to see maybe another pile of pinecones. But no such treasure was to be had this night.

She did, however, catch the reflection of light on an object lying by the door that she hadn't noticed when she first came out. Bending to have a closer look, Heddi gasped in surprise as she picked it up. It was an old red dog tag of Cooper's that he had lost on their hike in the woods last Christmas. Heddi had bought the bone shaped tag engraved with his name that year and put it in Cooper's stocking. Their hike that day had been the first and only time he had worn it.

Somewhere on the hike, it must have snagged on a branch and come loose. Neither Heddi nor Charlie had noticed until they were back home. They had looked for that tag on every hike they had taken since, but to no avail. Now here it was, suddenly sitting on her front porch. As Heddi rubbed crusty mud off the tag that so reminded her of her beloved lost friend, she started to feel as if Cooper was right there beside her, trying to tell her something. "Ok Heddi. Better give your head a shake," she told herself. "This whole light thing is making you a little crazy!" But the fact that the tag was there was very real, and Heddi couldn't simply ignore it. She had read numerous stories about dogs who had tried to communicate with their loved ones after they had passed away. Maybe Cooper *was* right here, and maybe he was trying to tell *her* something. "Well, you better polish up your communicating skills, old fella," she out loud. 'Cause this old granny is having some trouble getting the message!" She took the tag inside and placed it in the same bowl that she had used to hold the mysterious pinecones.

Chapter 4

"Naaana!" Kristen had dropped Missy off while she went to the store and Heddi knew exactly what her little granddaughter's first question would be. "Are we going to decorate today?" Heddi supposed there would be no delaying the inevitable. Today she would have to venture back into the depths of the storage room, and pull out the Christmas boxes. At least with little Miss Chatterbox helping her, it would be a lively undertaking. Sure enough, Missy was no more than through the door when she asked where the decorations were. When Heddi told her that they were still in the storage room, her little face fell. "But Nana! You said we would decorate this week!"

"And we will," Heddi assured her. "In fact, what do you say we head in there right now and get started?" Missy clapped her hands together, and jumped up and down in agreement, blonde curls bobbing to the beat. "Let's go Nana!" she shouted, taking Heddi's hand and leading the way. Box after box came out of the closet and was dragged into the living room. "You sure do have a lot of decorations!" Missy declared. Heddi laughed. "Yes, I do. Your Papa and I have had all these decorations since your Mommy was a little girl."

"Did Mommy used to help you decorate when she was little?" Missy queried.

"She certainly did," Heddi answered. "Your Mama always insisted that we decorate as soon as the first day of December rolled around. I think your Mama loved Christmas more than anyone else in the whole family! That's why your house is always decorated before any of the others on your street!"

"And I love Christmas, too!" Missy declared. Heddi laughed and gave her a big hug. They spent a wonderful afternoon chatting over the boxes of decorations. At four, Missy's idea of decorating meant mostly pulling things out of the box until it was empty and then moving on to the next one. There really wasn't a lot of actual decorating done, but her delight at discovering each intriguing decoration that she hadn't seen for a whole year was like a treasure hunt full of wonderful surprises. Very soon they had wound up every windup toy, shook every snow globe, played every music box and watched every animated creation go through its routine. By the time Kristen arrived back from getting a few groceries, Heddi's coffee table, kitchen table, and much of the floor was covered with a bright array of Charismas ornaments, animated figurines, nativity scenes, candles, wreaths as well as an assortment of pillows and throws that Heddi knew Cooper would have claimed had he still been with them. He had always had a fondness for the small lap quilt she kept folded on the back of the loveseat. If no one was watching he would grab a corner of the quilt in his teeth and ever so gently pull it to the floor where he would proceed to make a comfy little nest for a nap. Heddi felt a pang as she remembered how cute Cooper and Charlie had looked curled up for a winter's day nap, Charlie under the Christmas afghan and Cooper on top of the Christmas quilt.

Heddi was startled from her remembering by the thump of the screen door closing. As Kristen stepped carefully through the chaos of Heddi's living room, she apologized. "I guess you didn't actually get much decorating done with little miss helpful here, did you?"

"We had a wonderful time," Heddi replied. "Missy helped me get everything out so I could see what I had so I could decide where I wanted to put everything."

Kristen laughed. "Oh, I'm sure she did. Now let's get busy actually putting some of it where it belongs." Kristen found a Christmas CD in amongst all the mess and loaded it into Heddi's player. For the next couple of hours they all sang along while they put out all the decorations. When things finally looked pretty good, Heddi suggested it was time for some cookies and hot chocolate. "Not cookies," declared Missy. "Popcorn! With lots of butter! That's what you're 'posed to eat with hot chocolate when you're decorating!" Heddi and Kristen both laughed. At just four, Missy was already the enforcer of tradition. Charlie had always made a big bowl of buttered popcorn whenever they decorated and Missy wasn't about to let things change. Heddi went to the kitchen to prepare the snack while Kristen and Missy tidied away the empty boxes. Once the room was back to normal, Kristen noticed the bowl of pinecones in the center of the coffee table. With just a touch of surprise and pleasure in her voice, she asked Heddi if she had been out in the woods to gather pinecones for the verandah. Kristen knew what a tradition it had always been for her Mom and Dad, and she was happy to think that her Mom was going to continue with the tradition on her own. "Did you get them in the woods or just on the short trail?" she asked. Heddi hesitated for just a moment and with a bit of a troubled sigh, began relaying the story of the mysterious pinecones to her daughter. She also pointed out the battered red tag that sat in the dish along with them. She deliberately left out the part where she thought she saw a dog just like Cooper running up the driveway. At her age, she didn't need her children starting to worry about her mental capacities. Just having to tell them about the pinecones was bad enough. At least a squirrel or some other rodent could explain their appearance to some extent. It was a little harder to explain the dog tag, but it could just have resurfaced from its hiding place on its own. After all, she wasn't one hundred percent sure that it had been lost on the trail. For all she knew, Cooper may have simply lost it in the garden and it had worked its way onto the porch from there. Best to leave it at that for the kid's sake anyway. Kristen seemed genuinely concerned when Heddi mentioned Drew's comments about the coyotes. She too, advised her Mom to take plenty of precautions when venturing outside at night. To appease Kristen, Heddi agreed to be careful, but she knew in her heart that some other force was at work here, and she was pretty sure it wasn't coyotes. She wouldn't have admitted it, but suddenly she was kind of looking forward to the evening to see if any new objects appeared. She found herself feeling almost an anticipation rather than fear, as if she was going to make a connection with the loving and loyal companion that she missed so much.

They said their goodbyes at the door with promises of getting at the outdoor decorating when and if Heddi decided to do it. Once Heddi had seen them off, she returned inside to make her own dinner. At least cooking for one and eating dinner on her own wasn't a new experience for her. Charlie had travelled a lot for his work and Heddi had always worked hard to still prepare healthy family meals. It was a habit that she continued even after they had become empty nesters and Charlie was still travelling. He used to worry that she would stop eating well when he was away, but she had reassured him that that was not the case. Not only did she enjoy the challenge of thinking up good dinner ideas for one, she also saw it as an opportunity to enjoy some of the foods that she enjoyed but Charlie did not. There weren't many, as Charlie had always been an avid food lover, but there were a few. At any rate, tonight she really didn't feel much like cooking and there was some homemade soup left from the day before. That and some toast would suit her just fine.

As the darkness outside deepened, Heddi began to wonder if her ghostly guest would make another appearance. She hadn't really admitted these feelings of other worldly forces being at work here until today, and now she was referring to her visitor as a ghost! Heddi laughed to herself, wondering what others would think if they knew. She even found herself considering a plan to stay by the window for the evening so she could be right there the second the motion light came on.

"But you might sit there all night and have nothing happen," said a more rational voice inside her head. *"You might sit there for hours only to have your visitor come when you take two minutes to go to the bathroom or answer the phone. Better get a grip, Heddi, and abandon this plan!"*

Heddi shook her head at the conversation she was having with herself. She warmed her soup, buttered her toast and retreated to the TV room where she had no direct view of the front porch. If the light came on, she wouldn't even know, and perhaps that was a much better strategy. Heddi enjoyed her supper along with one of her favorite shows. At its end, she decided she would run a hot bath and relax for a while before bed. On her way to the bathroom, she couldn't help but pause at the front door and take a peek around the porch. She couldn't see anything unusual or out of place, no strange objects sitting around, and no unexpected treasures waiting to be discovered. As Heddi turned away to run her bath, she realized she was actually a little disappointed. Ghostly or not, feeling like she was connecting with Cooper had been a pleasant distraction from the sorrow that hung so heavy over her nights. Heddi knew that time was the best healer and that it wasn't something that could be hurried. As she sank into the bubbles, Missy's words about Papa not liking her to be sad popped into her head. "I'll try harder too, Papa," she said out loud. The warm water and aromatic bubbles worked their magic and Heddi dozed off for a while.

Quite some time later, dressed in fuzzy pj's and a robe, Heddi headed for the kitchen to make her tea. As she came out of the bathroom she was startled to see that the porch light was on. Heddi headed eagerly for the front door and opened it without even looking out first. There was, of course, nothing there. Except for tonight's treasure. Lying there, just as the dog tag had been, was another rusty long forgotten item. This time it was an old cookie cutter in the shape of a Christmas tree. As Heddi bent to pick it up, she thought back to the last time she had seen it. She had given it to Missy to use in the sandbox one day when she was making mud pies. It was quite dull and bent out of shape, so Heddi said she could have it. That had to easily be two years ago. Missy hadn't played in the sandbox much since she had learned to ride first a trike and then a bike with training wheels. Now this rusty cutter had mysteriously appeared at her doorstep. Heddi wondered about its' possible significance. She had always done a lot of Christmas baking for friends and family. A decorative cookie tin filled with goodies was her favorite gift to give teachers, the mail driver, the nurses at the clinic and various other folks in the community that were so helpful to her and Charlie throughout the year. Charlie had never really been involved in much of the baking, but he had always helped with the packaging. Making things look pretty was one of his special talents. He could create a marvelous gift basket or wrap an awesome present, where as Heddi fumbled with such tasks, claiming she was neither creative enough or patient enough to make things look that good. That was about the only connection she could make to this newest trinket and the Christmas season. Was Cooper trying to tell her that it was about time to get baking? Now that she thought about it, Cooper had always been right at her feet while she baked, waiting for bits and pieces of sugary goodness to fall to the floor. And then there were his own Christmas cookies, of course! Heddi slapped herself on the forehead. How could she not have seen it? She also used to bake healthy dog cookies that she and Cooper delivered every year to the local animal shelter and clinic to share a bit of Christmas spirit with the animals staying there over the holidays. Heddi hadn't done that yet this year either. With Cooper not around, she had simply forgotten all about it. Heddi carried the rusty old cookie cutter into the house and placed it in the dish with the other items.

Her heart was heavy and her head full of guilt for the traditions she had neglected. She just didn't feel like doing all those things by herself. Why didn't Cooper understand that? How could he want her to try and still do all the things that they loved to do together when he wasn't there to share them? Why was he letting her find these reminders of the good times right when she was already struggling to simply keep herself together?

Heddi stared at the objects sitting in the basket on the table. As she pondered the unusual combination of items, she started to smile through her tears. "Oh I think I'm starting to understand," she whispered with a nod of her head.

It was hard to understand, and harder still to believe, but somehow, after already giving her a lifetime of love and loyalty, Cooper had found a way to give her one final gift. The gift of healing. Now Heddi understood that the key to being happy again had to begin with embracing the traditions that they had always enjoyed rather than abandoning them.

The pine cones were a reminder that she needed to decorate the verandah just as they had always done so that she would enjoy the glow of the lights whenever she returned home from an outing. To not do so would mean a dark gloomy return that would only result in dark gloomy feelings, thus extending her grief and making the healing even harder.

The rusty dog tag was a reminder that it was important to continue her walks in the woods, even if she had to go alone. It was good for her body and good for her soul. It too, would help her to heal.

The rusty cookie cutter served as a reminder that sometimes traditions were kept in order to help others enjoy a happier season, as was the case with her gifts of yummy goodness. Heddi knew that giving to others was always the best way to make yourself feel better. Why had she not thought about that this Christmas?

Suddenly Heddi knew what she had to do. "I'll start tomorrow," she promised out loud to a Cooper she was sure was listening, eyes alert and head tilted to one side. Tomorrow I'll go and collect the pine cones and boughs to decorate the verandah. Then I'll start baking all the favorite cookies that you and I enjoyed sharing. Then, after all the Christmas festivities are over, the "three" of us will go for a nice long hike in the woods.

"Thank you Cooper. Have I got it right?" Heddi smiled. If Cooper could somehow work his magic to help her understand what she needed to do, the least she could do is have a conversation with him. She could almost hear his enthusiastic "woof" in reply. Her heart ached so much with a longing to touch his soft warm fur and bury her face in the scruff of his neck. Heddi truly believed that one day they would be reunited, but for now, just feeling this special connection would have to do.

That evening, when Heddi's light came on yet again, she wondered what gift Cooper could possibly be bringing her this time. Though there was nothing there, and no mysterious treasures appeared, a sudden feeling of warmth and contentment filled her heart as she gazed out into the winter night. Then, as she stood watching the soft snow begin to fall, she was certain that she saw the fading shadows of a man and a dog walking off into the darkness and she smiled.

"Merry Christmas my loves", she whispered. It would be a wonderful Christmas after all!

The End

CONNECTED
Souls

DANA LANDERS

CONNECTED SOULS

BY

Dana Landers

©2012

ALL RIGHTS RESERVED

TABLE OF CONTENTS

Note from the author

Although this short story is a work of fiction, it is based on a true story from my own life. I believe that quite often dogs that we have loved and that have loved us return to us in different forms. With this belief, I carry the memory of each and every one of the dogs that I have loved in my heart forever. At the time of this writing Riley is curled up beside me where I hope he will be for some time to come.

On Feb. 10, a dog named Cujo was surrendered to the Westfield animal shelter. Also on Feb 10. in a Westfield home, a dog named Codi said his final goodbye to the family he had loved for over 10 years. This is the story of their connected souls.

Chapter 1: Codi

It had been a long day of whining, grumpy kids. Providing home daycare was a job that Karen usually loved, but today had been one of those days that made her wonder if she wasn't getting too old for it all. She was over 50, after all! And she had been doing this job for nearly thirty years! She also knew that a lot of how she was feeling had to do with it being winter and the fact that everybody was suffering from a bit of cabin fever. Just the same, whatever the reason, it was starting to wear her down. But as it did every day, the hands of the clock finally made their way to 6 and the last tired child was sent off in the loving arms of equally weary parents. "Just a bit of clean up to do," Karen thought to herself, and she could begin her evening.

The first thing on the agenda every night was a walk with Codi, her Spaniel, Border collie cross. He was a shaggy little thing, all brown, black and white fur, with a long tail, floppy ears and short stocky legs. The kids had picked him from the litter for just that reason. They laughed at how his little legs couldn't even get him up the first steps of the front porch. They also loved his chubby little puppy belly which he had somehow never managed to outgrow.

But short legs or not, he was always ready for a walk, and he did his best to make sure it was never forgotten. For that reason alone, Karen's daily routine seldom changed. Every night after she shut off the lights, closed the door and headed upstairs from the daycare, he would be in the exact same spot. She knew he would be there, waiting at the top of the stairs, stretched out with front paws dangling down over the top step, nosed pressed against the gate, tail sweeping a clean spot across the hardwood floor, and eyes bright with anticipation.

"Are we going now?" he seemed to say. "I've been waiting for you. Let's go."

And regardless of how tired she was, or what kind of a day it had been, she couldn't resist those eyes. She would bundle up for the cold and snow while Codi watched and waited. He never seemed to quite understand what took her so long or why she had to put on so many things in order to go out when he was always at the ready to just run out the door.

"If I had your fur coat," she would say, "I could just walk out the door too!"

But he would wait patiently knowing that eventually she would be ready. It was with these thoughts in mind that Karen finally flicked off the last light switch and closed the downstairs door. As she came around the landing to head upstairs, she was surprised to see that Codi wasn't there. "Where are you old fellow?" she called. "This winter weather got you down too? Am I going to get a reprieve from walking today?"

When even her cheerful comments didn't bring him to the top of the stairs, Karen began to worry. At 10, Codi was getting on and he had been moving a bit slower these past few months. The deep, thawing snow posed a particularly difficult challenge for his short little legs this time of year. At times she would almost have to lift his back end out of the snow if he sank down too far. But he was a determined fellow, and he loved his walks! So it was quite natural for Karen to be concerned when he wasn't waiting there ready to go. Karen continued to the top of the stairs and unlatched the child gate at the top.

"Codi!" she called. "Ready for a walk?" Now she could see him. He was lying in the center of the carpet looking at her and wagging his tail but making no move to get up. "What's wrong Codi? Come here boy. It's walk time." Karen tapped her leg in a typical come here motion. The response she received was not at all what she had hoped for. She watched with dismay as Codi tried to stand up and come to her. Struggle as he might, he couldn't get up on all four legs. He could drag his back end but he couldn't stand. His eyes were still the same, full of hope and anticipation but there was something else there too, a sadness maybe, or perhaps an apology. Like he was trying to tell her that he wasn't going to be able to make it this time; that things weren't going to be the same anymore. Karen fell to her knees beside him, stroking his head and feeling the tears start to come.

"Oh buddy, what's happened? You were fine this morning. You were fine when I let you out this afternoon." Karen just sat there on the floor for the longest time, crying and petting her beloved companion. When Will, her husband came in from work, that is how he found them. Trying not to cry, Karen explained the situation and Will called their vet at the Westfield Animal Hospital. Dr. Jameson agreed to see them, and made the arrangements for Codi to come in for an emergency examination. Karen's heart sank as she watched Will carry that furry ball of love out to the car. She knew it was bad. She felt it down to the depths of her soul. And she knew that Codi felt it too. In just the blink of an eye, things were suddenly so different. There was no denying the fact that life was going to change tonight forever.

Will returned in less than an hour. He carried Codi in and placed him on his bed in the corner of the living room. The news was every bit as bad as Karen had known it would be. Dr. Jameson had told Will that a nerve was severed in Codi's spine and that his back legs could no longer function. It was possible, he said, that the strain of walking through the deep snow may have accelerated a condition that had already began to progress. Or it may have happened suddenly one time when he slipped trying to get up. There was no way to ever know for sure. The fact of the matter was, he couldn't stand, couldn't walk, and basically couldn't get around except by dragging his back end. The good news was that he was not in any pain. Surgery was an option, albeit a very expensive one, and would require the amputation of both back legs. Codi would then need to be fitted for a custom cart that would hold up his back end and roll forward as he moved his front legs. It seemed like a very complicated and unnatural way to move.

The vet was blunt and told Karen and Will to consider very carefully what Codi's quality of life would be like. And in addition to all of that, there was Codi's age to consider. Also, as Dr. Jameson pointed out, Codi had never quite been back to normal from the bladder stone surgery he had had the year before. His system was not as good as it might need to be to face surgery. The vet was being honest when he told them of the risks of the surgery and the chance that Codi's system would not be able to withstand the stress. The other option, of course, was putting Codi down. Neither Karen nor Will wanted to make that final call. They had been down this road before but never had they ended up there so suddenly and without any mental preparation. This time there was no lengthy illness or failing health to give them some time to adjust to what was coming. This time they had to make the call even when everything else about their beloved friend seemed perfectly fine. Everything except the fact that he could no longer walk!

But in the end, to do their best by their faithful, loyal friend, that was the decision they made.

They made the appointment for the following morning and took Codi home for one last goodbye from the rest of the family. The ride home was quiet and their hearts were heavy. This would be their last night together. Once they were in and had Codi settled on a blanket in the living room, Karen started making calls to her daycare parents. Daycare would be cancelled for the next day. Fortunately it was a Friday, so the weekend would be free as well. With business matters taken care of, they sat quietly together reminiscing about Codi's puppy days, his antics growing up, and all the wonderful ways in which he had enriched their lives. One by one the children went off to bed and Karen and Will sat with Codi a while longer. It was difficult getting him outside to relieve himself, but they did their best. Cody knew things weren't right. He sensed the sadness that now filled the house that was usually so happy and he knew that he was the reason. He tried with his eyes to let them know that everything would be ok. That they were making the right decision and one that he was grateful for. He so wished he could talk to them and tell them that he was looking forward to crossing over the Rainbow Bridge. He was full of anticipation of things to come. But he wanted to tell them too, that he was sorry to be leaving them. He also wanted to somehow let them know, that even though he would no longer be with them as the dog they knew, he would be with them still through the spirit of a dog that they were soon to know.

But sadly, dogs have no voice for human language. So he lay quietly, accepting their hugs and scratches, returning their love as best he could with a gentle lick of the hand or a paw resting on their leg. It was a long, strange night for Codi and his family, one of the longest Karen could remember. But when morning came, they went together to say their final goodbyes.

Chapter 2: Cujo

It was just before 9 when Becky drove into the parking lot of the Westfield animal shelter. A light winter rain was falling and coated her windshield between swooshes of the wipers. As she got closer, her stomach tightened at the sight of the large crate sitting beside the door. "Looks like we have another one," she said to herself. Though she had worked at the shelter for over eight years, she never got used to the way people could just abandon an animal that they had owned and cared for.

She didn't understand why people couldn't at least bring the dogs into the shelter instead of just dropping them off when the shelter was closed. There was never enough information about the surrendered animal when they did it this way. There would be so little information to pass along to perspective new owners. Nothing about his personality that would help match him up with the right family. Nothing, either good or bad that they could use to help make him more adoptable, to increase his chances of finding that perfect, happy forever home that he so deserved. Nothing. Just a few words scratched on a piece of paper. Sometimes they didn't even get that. It was always so sad when it happened this way.

She hoped he had only been there a while and not all night. She opened the car door and walked slowly towards the large wire cage "Hello there big guy," Becky said in a calm voice, as she approached the cage. "Aren't you a handsome fellow?" He was a fairly large dog and obviously of mixed breed. He sported black, brown and white markings very similar to a Bernese mountain dog, but with a more slender build. His nose looked almost like that of a German shepherd, but his ears were all floppy like a retriever. He was tall with a long black tail and fuzzy tan britches. The most unusual thing about him was the one ear that sat sideways atop his head as though it had forgotten which way to go. It gave the dog a very bewildered look that made you want to hug him all the more. "Well now," said Becky, "Let's just see what this note says about you."

Scrawled on a small piece of paper tied to the wire crate were these few words: "This dogs' name is Cujo. He is almost a year old and just got too big for our house and our kids. I hope you can find him a good home. Thanks."

That's it. That's all she wrote. Becky sighed and looked into the sad brown eyes and wondered what his story really was, and why on earth anyone would name a family pet Cujo! He certainly looked anything but mean or aggressive.

"Oh well," she thought. "Doesn't really matter. From here on in it's you and me and the rest of the staff. And hopefully, soon a new home with new owners."

There was a long red leash attached to the black collar around the dog's neck. Becky talked to him for a bit just to judge his reaction to her presence. When it appeared he was going to be quite docile, she slowly opened the door of the crate, talking in a reassuring tone the whole time. Cujo made no move to exit the crate, even when Becky tugged gently on the leash and urged him to come. It was obvious he had trust issues and was afraid of new situations. Becky knew that patience would be the key. She just kept talking and gradually came close enough to pat his head. When he immediately drew back, Becky did too.

"Ok fella," she said, "nobody here is going to hurt you. Let's just get you out of this crate and inside the shelter." She wanted to get him in and settled before all the staff started to arrive. She had a sense that the chatter and bustle of everyone coming in might really scare this poor guy. With a bit more coaxing she was able to get him to walk with her. They stopped briefly by the walk and Cujo relieved himself on the bushes. "There you go," said Becky. "See, everything is ok. You are going to be fine. We're going to take really good care of you."

Cujo was glad to get out of the crate and stretch. He had been scared and cold sitting there all by himself, wondering if anyone was going to come. Even when his people had shut him in the small room every day, it had not been as lonely as being outside in the cold dark of early morning. He wondered where his people had gone, and why they had left him here. Would they return to take him home soon? Didn't they want him anymore? He had tried to be a good dog. He had stayed quiet in the small space every day, never barking or scratching at the door. He even tried not to urinate if he could help it, but sometimes the days were just too long and he had to go. When that happened, he always went to the farthest corner of the small place, and only as often as was absolutely necessary. He never wanted to make his people unhappy.

Lately, though, he had heard the woman person complaining that he was getting too big. He had always felt in his heart that she was unhappy with him, and kind of angry with the man for bringing him home. "He is way too big to play with the kids now," she would say. "And way too big for this tiny house." This made him very sad. He loved to play with his kids and always tried to be extra careful. But maybe he hadn't been careful enough. Maybe the woman person had finally had enough and now they had left him here.

He didn't know where or what this place was, but this kind girl who was taking him out of the crate seemed very nice and gentle. Her soft voice was comforting and he wasn't afraid of her at all. The room where she took him was warm, and bright. It was clean and yet still smelled of lots of other dogs and animals. He was somewhat confused by the feelings that were coming at him from the other dogs. There seemed to be both a sense of hope and of sadness.

Later during his time here, he would learn the reason for those two emotions. There was a sense of gladness for those friends that had moved on to new homes and families, and a sorrowful kind of hope for those who were granted passage to a different place. Although their lives here on this earth had been cut short, they would now able to move forward to a new place; a place where they could begin their journey across the rainbow bridge to the land where all dogs live free from worry, illness and pain. Cujo knew that it was his time now to sit and wait. In the end, it would be one or the other of those same fates that would be his. For now, though, he was happy to be safe, warm and cared for in what he chose to call his "in between" place. The place he heard others refer to as "the shelter."

Chapter 3: Grieving

It was a warm day for mid February and raining lightly when Karen
and Will pulled into the animal hospital parking lot. The smell of
spring was in the air, a smell that usually brought a sense of new
beginnings and anticipation of summer. But not today. Today it
seemed unfair that the weather should be so nice. A bitter cold
blustery day would better suit their mood for sure. When they
arrived at the hospital, Karen stood in the rain and talked to Codi
through the opened back hatch of their SUV. He was curled up on
his favorite blanket sniffing in great gulps of the spring like air.

His eyes never left Karen's as they tried so hard to communicate
their last thoughts to each other. Codi wanted her to know that he
was ok. That this was how things were meant to be, and that soon,
they would find themselves comforted by the love of a new canine
companion.

Karen wanted Codi to know how much she loved him, would
always love him; and that he had done a wonderful job as a friend,
guardian and companion. She stroked his head gently and waited
for Will to return. He had gone ahead to find out where the vet
wanted them to take Codi with as little exposure as possible to the
other waiting patients and their owners.

Will returned shortly and said it was time. He gently lifted Codi
from the blanket and carried him inside to a quiet room. Karen
grabbed Codi's blanket and followed, eyes down, not wanting to
look at the other dogs that were there. Other dogs that would be
going home with their owners today to continue their normal lives.
She followed Will into the office. Codi was placed on his blanket on
the table. The vet spoke to them briefly, explaining with genuine
compassion, how things would happen, and what to expect. He
explained how Codi would receive two injections. One now, to
relax and calm him, and a final one which would stop his heart. The
vet administered the first needle and then left them alone with Codi

for a few moments to say their final goodbyes. When he returned, second needle in hand, he asked if they were ready. Will nodded and the doctor looked to Karen. Tears began to fall as Karen nodded her ok. Then she knelt at Codi's head and looked straight into his eyes as the final needle was delivered. Karen watched as Codi's eyes began to droop, just as they always had when he dropped off to sleep. He opened them one last time after the final needle was given. Karen could feel his love and knew that he felt hers. She stroked his head and sobbed as his eyes closed once again for the last time. She continued to pet him while the vet used a stethoscope to check his heart. She laid her head against his, her tears wetting the soft brown fur, as the vet's words stabbed into her heart. "Codi's gone," he said quietly.

Since they had made previous arrangements to have his ashes returned to them for private burial, there was no further business to attend to. Dr. Jameson left them alone then, saying to take as much time as they needed, and to feel free to leave via the back door whenever they were ready. They remained with Codi for some time, hating so much to leave him there. Eventually they gently removed his collar and gave him one last hug. It was over. "Thank you, Codi," Karen whispered. "Thank you for a job well done. We'll never forget you. Be happy, now. Goodbye dear friend."

For a good part of that day, Karen walked and walked in the rain, hardly aware that she was soaked right through. The cold and discomfort matched her mood. She knew that only time would ease the pain, but for now she accepted the heartache.

Chapter 4: Back at the shelter

After only a few days, Cujo found himself settling in quite nicely at the shelter. In fact, he rather enjoyed the freedom of his large kennel and his daily walks with gentle, caring people. Some of them worked at the shelter and some came in every now and then. The other dogs told him they were called volunteers, and that they came to visit the dogs here just to make them feel loved. Cujo had never known so many people who freely offered such kind words and frequent scratches behind the ears. He was so thankful not to be locked in that small space anymore. He still missed his people, however, especially his kids. But he had come to accept that they wouldn't be taking him home ever again. His heart felt a little sad by this, much as it had felt when he was taken from his mother and his sisters at the farm. It only hurt really bad for a while and then with time, you began to forget. You moved on and learned what was expected of you in your new life. Cujo wondered what his new life would be like after the shelter. Would he find new people in a forever home this time? Someone to love him as much as he wanted to love. Someone he could protect and stand by for all of his days? Cujo knew again, that only time would tell. What he didn't know, was how short a time he really had for that to happen.

Most dogs were only kept at the shelter for a few weeks. And for Cujo the clock had begun ticking down. Lots of people came to the shelter to look for new companions. Once a little girl and her dad took Cujo for a walk and stayed to pet him for quite a while. The little girl was just the kind of friend Cujo would love to have. He would walk by her side, sleep by her bed and take care of her in every way a dog could. He was so hopeful that they would take him home. But in the end, he heard those same human words that he had heard before. "He's just too big." He never saw the little girl again.

For several more long days, there were no visitors that stopped by Cujo's crate. He enjoyed hearing the other dogs bark with happiness as they left with happy new owners; for a dog knows no such thing as envy or jealousy, only joy for the good fortune of others. Maybe soon it would be his turn.

Chapter 5: Moving on

Karen couldn't believe that two weeks had passed since they had lost Codi. She still felt him with her everywhere; in the car, at home, even when she walked down the street. At times, she swore she could hear his nails click clacking across the floor. She would turn, almost expecting to see him there. She still expected to see him standing at the top of the stairs when she finished her day, wagging his tail and waiting patiently for his walk. But she also knew that the pain was growing softer. She could talk about him now without crying, at least. She could laugh with family members about some of the crazy things he had done. She knew she was healing. And she knew that she was starting to miss having a dog around. Will had asked her several times if she was ready to start thinking about another dog, but until now, Karen had been emphatic in her refusal. Until now, it had seemed too soon. It had seemed somehow disloyal to Codi. But Karen was beginning to sense a change. Some little voice was telling her it was time to move on, that maybe there was another dog out there that needed her and the love she had to give. And then she had the dream. It was just her and Codi in the dream. They were walking and playing as they always had, happy and smiling, but there was one big difference. Codi was entirely white. In the dream, Karen seemed oblivious to this fact. She knew only that Codi was running with her like he had as a puppy, tail wagging and short little legs trying to keep up. Karen awoke with such a feeling of contentment and peace. Although she only told close family members about the dream, she believed it was an omen. A sign from Codi that it was time to move on. Maybe today she would suggest to Will that they just go see what dogs were at the shelter. "I don't know for sure, that I'm ready," Karen said. "But let's just go see. I just have a feeling that maybe we are meant to go today." When they arrived at the shelter, they asked about the dogs that were available for adoption. As the girl described several of the dogs, Karen listened but didn't feel like any of them sounded quite right. Until she spoke of one particular rescue. "We do have a dog who was surrendered about two weeks ago," she said as she read from a clipboard of papers. He was left here February 10 by his previous owners. Karen heard very little of her next words, struck by the fact that this dog had been surrendered on the very day that they had had to put Codi down. Karen felt sure that this was the connection she was waiting for. This was the dog they were meant to have. "We would like to see that dog," Karen said. "He sounds perfect!"

Chapter 6: The Connection

The days moved on, and as much as he was comfortable at the shelter, Cujo began to feel very restless. He sensed that something new was coming his way. Then one day he felt an unusual sadness mixed with an odd kind of happiness in his belly. Something was different. He didn't understand what it was or where it was coming from but he knew that it meant there was a change coming for him. Somehow, somewhere the spirit of an unknown comrade was calling to him, telling him that soon, he would find his place and continue some very important work.

Sure enough, later that same day, a middle aged couple came to the shelter. They seemed to walk directly to his crate, bypassing several other dogs that wagged and wiggled and jumped and barked to get their attention. There was a sadness surrounding them, but it was tempered with a glimmer of hope and need. The woman person looked deep into his eyes and Cujo felt an immediate connection. This was the person he was meant to take care of. This was the person that his spirit companion was leading him to. Somehow he had to let her know that they were meant to be together. Since he was in the crate, he couldn't approach her and lean up against her to show his affection, so he did what he could. As she offered her hand through the bars of the crate, he licked it ever so gently, trying to show his love. Cujo watched as a different sensation appeared in the woman's eyes. It was love for sure and Cujo's heart almost burst. The couple left then, and Cujo was worried that they might not return. But the very next day the woman was back. She came alone this time to see him again. She stayed for only a short while but promised him that everything was going to be ok. He was going to be their dog and he was going to have the best life ever.

Sure enough, a few days later, the man person returned and Cujo was led out of his crate and into the care of the friendly, gentle man. He rode in the back seat of the car and he felt so wonderful. He was going to his forever home and he knew it. He could feel the spirit of the dog who had sat right here before him. He could feel all the positive love and energy that filled the air. As soon as he entered the house and met the woman person again, he knew he had absolutely nothing to fear. The spirit of the other dog was still here, waiting to pass the task of caring for his people over to Cujo. Cujo accepted the responsibility eagerly and made a promise to his departed companion that he would be loyal, loving and true to this family for all of his days on this earth. With that, the other spirit moved on and Cujo felt a happiness unlike anything he had ever felt before.

As the days went by, Cujo began to learn the routines and habits of the household. He was no longer called Cujo, but was renamed Riley. His people had smiled and made a joke about him having the "life of Riley." He didn't really know what that meant, but somehow he knew it was good.

And so it was. Riley lived out his life with the couple who had loved and cared for so many other dogs in their time. He continued the work that Codi and the others before him had begun. He was happy and content. He had found his forever home and it would be his until the time came to pass the job along to someone else. He hoped that day was a long way off.

The End

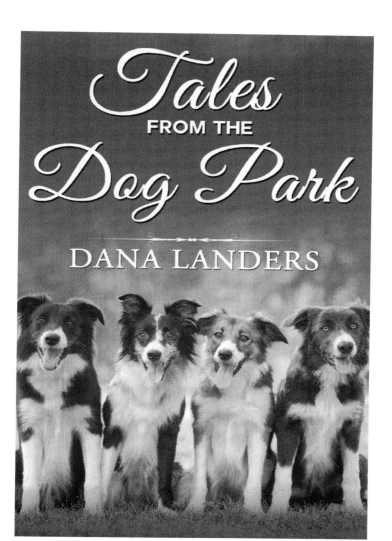

Tales From the Dog Park
(dog stories as told by Riley)

In Connected Souls, you were introduced to Cujo, the shelter dog who was adopted and renamed Riley. Riley has been living it up with his loving owners for over 12 years, and is now enjoying his golden years napping on the couch and reflecting on his life experiences. He still visits the local dog park every day where he likes to share his stories with the other dogs who gather there. These are some of those stories.

I am Riley

It's a typical day at the dog park. Dogs of all shapes and sizes are running around, noses to the ground sniffing. I once heard an owner compare this behavior to something humans do called "reading the paper." I guess they think it's how we gather the latest news on the who, what, and where of dog society. At any rate, I have come to the dog park as I do every day, to sniff, greet and to share. But before I begin, let me tell you a bit about myself.

I am Riley. Perhaps you met me previously in a book called Connected Souls which is the story my owner wrote about my very beginning time. But in case you haven't met me before, let me say again I am Riley.

I am a rescue dog. My owners, Karen and Will took me home from the shelter to give me the "Life of Riley" as they say. I am indeed a blessed dog. I have moved with my people several times and each and every time they included me in all the preparations and decisions. They made sure each home had a good yard for me and places where I could walk and chase my Frisbee. Every time we moved, my toys, blankets and bed were carefully packed so I would never have to be without them. I am well fed. In fact, my human "Mom", Karen, cooks homemade food for me every day, and bakes the tastiest treats ever!

The town where I currently live has a new dog park where my friends and I can all run free, without the hindrance of leash or collar. It's not a large area by any means, and it is entirely fenced so we are safe from danger. Naturally we would all prefer to run completely free and romp through the woods and fields, but that would surely make our humans anxious. These types of boundaries seem to help them relax while we run free, so we simply accept it as a good thing. We pay little notice to the fence anyway, as there are plenty of great trees to mark, long grass to chomp, and even a pond where we can cool off on hot days. We quite enjoy our daily romps there, and the young fellows always look to me to share dog stories and experiences from my life. I enjoy this, as I believe my wisdom and guidance may help some of the youngsters find their way in the human world a little easier. This book is an account of those stories. Hopefully human friends who read it will gain insight into the hearts and souls of the four legged companions who love them and want for nothing more than to make them happy.

Anyway, back to the dog park.

"Here he comes! Here he comes!" I hear their voices as I saunter towards the gated entry of the park. Before I am through the double gates, I can hear them start.

"Hey Riley! Got any good stories today?" I take a quick inventory of who is present today. My stories are often geared towards who is listening that day. You see, each of my friends is at a different stage of life and needs different things. With a quick read of the crowd, I see Jake, Chase, Max, Brandi and Tucker. Jake is a big black lab about 5 years old and full of endless energy. Chase is a small Sheltie who I often feel is much too vocal. Max is possibly my best friend. He is old, like me, a Shepherd Collie mix who's had some hard times and as a result is pretty aloof. I often have to work at getting him involved in the group. Brandi is a beautiful Golden Retriever. She reminds me of my dog Mom. She is gentle and patient and always listens with genuine interest to all of my stories. And finally, the remaining dog here today is Tucker. I have known Tucker almost all of my life. He was part of the family before I even came along. He visits our house often with his people and we are old pals. His human Mom and mine are sharing stories today too, while we dogs play. When I take a break from socializing with my canine friends, I love to listen to their conversation. They smile and laugh a lot and their happiness envelopes us all.

"Hey, Riley!" It's Jake making all the ruckus. "Got any good stories today?"

"In a minute, friends. A guy's gotta take care of business first." The others continue their sniffing and frolicking while I take my time tending to the usual daily routine. As I come up over the small hill at the back of the park, I see that a newcomer has arrived on the scene. The other dogs have all headed over to say hello and sniff their welcome. They completely encircle this poor creature who is quite obviously a little overwhelmed by all the sudden attention. The crowd spans out a bit as I approach, almost as if they want to give me my own chance to say hello. I smile to myself at the instant respect that old age commands.

The new dog is a medium sized mixed breed. By size, smell and behavior I guess him to be a mix of beagle and blue heeler. He is short legged, with mostly a beagle's markings except for areas where the fur is speckled. His eyes are round and, at the moment somewhat fearful. He looks tense; ready to run at any moment. I hear his owner calling him Boomer and encouraging him to "go play." I think Boomer needs a little help from a friend, so I step up.

"Ok guys. Let's give the little fella a bit of breathing room," I say and they all back away a bit. "New here to the dog park, are you? Well you have nothing to fear. These guys and gals may seem a bit crazy, but they're all friendly. They just get a bit excited when someone new joins the gang."

He seems to relax. I urge him to come take a walk around the park with me. Once we have lapped the park and he has sufficiently marked some territory, he begins to relax and interact with the others. He leaves my side now, and goes running after Jake and Brandi with Chance in hot pursuit. Tucker and Max, the old guys, hang back, as I do, and watch their fun. In our minds I know each one of us is remembering the good old days when we could run like that.

I remember a time too, when I was timid and afraid of the world just like Boomer. And I remember an incident that happened shortly after I came to live with Karen and Will. I can chuckle about it now, but at the time I thought for sure I was a dead dog. Maybe that will be the story for today.

And so our time at the dog park ends as it always does, with all the dogs spread out in the shade of the giant oak tree, listening to the stories that myself or one of the other old guys has to tell, while the owners chat and exchange dog stories of their own on the benches that are scattered throughout the park.

But anyway, like the title says, this book is about stories I tell. So let's get to them, shall we?

The Chase

You wouldn't know it to look at me today, but there was a time
when I could run like the wind. There wasn't a dog that could catch
me. It's a good thing too, because there was one day when I had to
run for my life!

You see, whenever we moved to a new house, Karen and Will
always made sure that there were plenty of places where I could go
for a free run off leash to get good exercise. Near this house, there
was an awesome cornfield with a tractor track that went
completely around the field. The farmer was a dog lover and had
no problems with dogs running free on the track, as long as we
stayed out of the corn field. We dogs were so grateful for a place to
run, we made sure never to go off the track. It was a great place to
run. The ground was packed down and level so we never had to
worry about stumbling into a hole or tripping in soft dirt. Most
days Karen took me to the field in the morning, and Karen and Will
took me together in the evenings. I really looked forward to those
runs. Naturally I could run a lot faster that my owners could walk,
so I used to run way up ahead to the bend in the track. Then,
because I couldn't see them anymore, I would turn around and run
full tilt all the way back to them! It was great fun!

I always had to walk to the field and home again on my leash
because there was a busy road to cross, gardens and green lawns to
avoid, and small children who were afraid of dogs to pass by. But
Karen and Will would always give me as much leash free time as
possible. But there was one day that I wished I had been on my
leash a little sooner.

We were just coming out from the bottom of the track to head
home. Karen and Will were chatting and I knew Will would be
clipping my leash on soon. I had wandered over to a particularly
interesting patch of long grass. There had been a dog there
recently whose scent I didn't recognize and I was trying to get a
good read on him. I must have been deep into sniffing because I
didn't see or hear the other dog coming until he was right on top of
me. I heard the snarl before I saw the face, and that was all it took
to make me move. This was not a friend coming to say hello, this
was a mean, aggressive fellow, who didn't like any other dogs
stepping on what he believed was his turf. I had never been in a
dog fight before, and had no desire to be in one now. I had seen
other dogs come through the shelter that had survived a fight or
two and believe me, it wasn't pretty. Let me tell you, at that

moment I was terrified. My first instinct was to run, and that's exactly what I did. I tucked my tail as low between my legs as I could and I turned on all the burners. I could hear Karen and Will's voices calling to me, and I could hear another man's voice calling another dog's name but I wasn't listening, just running. I could sense that I was running a lot faster than my foe, but I didn't slow down. I didn't really even look where I was going. I ran along the sidewalk so I could avoid the dangerous road, but I had no escape route in mind. I just kept going.

Suddenly something smelled and felt familiar. Home! It hadn't been our home for very long yet, but it had been long enough for me to recognize it. I made a beeline straight for the front porch, certain that I would be safe there. Finally, panting and exhausted, I stopped and sat on the top step. I knew no dog, no matter how vicious, would dare to attach me on my owner's property. I didn't need to worry, however, as I soon caught sight of my attacker secured on the leash of his man. The man was talking to Will and yanking hard on the dog's leash. Karen was hurrying towards me, looking worried and scared. It wasn't until I saw her expression that I thought about the risks I had taken crossing the busy road. I hadn't even thought about cars, or the danger they represented, all I wanted to do was get home.

In an instant Karen was on the step with me, hugging my neck and scratching my ears and telling me what a good dog I was to run home. Seems she was afraid I would just keep running, that she might never see me again. I realized then, how unsure they were that I loved them and trusted them. It was true that when they first brought me home, I had trust issues. After all, my first humans had been very mean to me. But I know love when I see it, and I knew these people loved me. And I think they know now, after today, that I love them. I proved to them that my place is with them and that anyplace where we all live together is home.

Frisbees

I realized a very strange thing at the dog park today. Just on the other side of our fence, there is an odd looking structure that humans play with. It is made of metal and chains and I've heard it referred to as a Frisbee golf basket. Apparently this is some type of game that humans play where they throw Frisbees into this basket. Now, I suppose, for humans this makes the game of Frisbee a bit more interesting, and that's all well and good. But what I can't understand, is why in the world they would build a Frisbee game for people right beside a park where dogs come to run and play. Don't they realize that all those Frisbees flying by on the other side of the fence creates pure torture for some of us? After all, if you're a Frisbee catching dog and you see Frisbees flying by, the only thing you want to do is catch them, right? It just makes sense! So some of my friends end up running up and down the edge of the dog park looking like dogs gone mad, running and barking and snapping at thin air. It keeps them busy I suppose, and certainly gets them their exercise, but for some, it's pretty annoying.

On the other hand, as far as the humans are concerned, it can sure be a little frustrating for players who have less than perfect aim too, because many of their Frisbees end up in the dog park. Now there are three pretty good reasons why this becomes a problem. One, if you don't happen to be a dog lover, you may be a little hesitant to head into a park that's full of free running dogs. And two, even if you love dogs a lot, you might not want to go chasing after some eighty pound lab who has claimed your Frisbee as his own. And three, maybe you don't really want your expensive game quality Frisbee embellished with dozens of tiny tooth marks, cause I'm pretty sure they won't help it to fly better!

At least the organizers of this strange activity had the foresight to put a gate from one area into the other so stray and captured Frisbees could, at least, be reclaimed.

It also put the idea of training Frisbee dogs into the head of many a dog owner who probably should have chosen a much different dog activity.

This was especially true of one of my park buddies, an energetic Aussie named Pete who was in no way quick enough, either in mind or body to be a good disc catcher. Time after time his owner would throw the disc. Time after time , Pete would watch it go sailing by over his head and then run to try and catch it. Needless to say, every time the disc would come down and Pete would either get hit on the head by it, trip over it or run clear on by it. Of course, he did always grab it in the end, and head back to his owner. But even then, he would stop several feet away and drop it, looking expectantly at his owner. Exasperated, his owner would urge him to at least bring it all the way back to him. They continued at this for several days with little progress. Then one day Pete arrived at the park with his lady human instead of the man. She was much more interested in socializing with the other owners and had no interest in playing catch. Pete, I guess, decided this would be a good time to ask the "old pro" how it was really done.

"Hey Riley!" "Can you give me a few pointers? I'd really like to do this thing for my owner. It seems to mean a lot to him."

"Why not?" I thought. "Might as well help the pup out a bit of I can. I was pretty good at it, even if I do say so myself. Mind you, I've had a lot of practice. Will started throwing them for me right from the beginning of our time together. At first he threw them only a short distance so I could get the idea, and then before long I was snatching them out of the air as far as he could throw them. It was a rare thing for me to miss one! But let me tell you, there is some technique to be learned if you want to do it right. So listen up, kiddo, and I'll give you some tips."

I have to hand it to the kid. He really paid attention. And from what I've seen lately, he's put it all into practice. On any given day now, you can catch a very exuberant Pete and a very proud man playing Frisbee catch together and loving every minute of it.

But that's how we dogs are. It's just in our nature to please our people and do whatever they expect from us. The real bonus comes when that something is a thing that we both enjoy and that strengthens the bond we share.

"Way to go, Pete!" "You do us all proud!"

Scary Things

It seems there are a few holidays every year where humans feel compelled to light up the sky with loud, scary lights that scare the fur off every dog I know. They call them " fireworks," and I have no idea what the attraction is. Some of them included really loud bangs and brilliant flashes of light. Some were a single flash followed by a sound I called the "zipper'" It made me feel as though some giant dog devouring creature was going to descend from the sky and carry me away.

For most of us animals, anything that has anything at all to do with fire is something to be avoided at all costs. Unless of course, it involves a cozy fireplace with a nice soft rug in front! Even then, we respect this fire and are prepared to take flight at any moment in case that fire escapes its place. But these exploding, blazing sky fires are something we simply can't accept.

Now some of you young fellows want to know how I deal with these things. Fortunately for me, my people have realized how upsetting these events are for me, and they leave me at home whenever they go to see them. If your people haven't quite got that message yet, be patient. They will learn. Soon they will realize that your trembling bones, and racing heart are for real and they'll leave you at home too. If, for some reason, these events take place within your own territory, and you can't avoid them, here are some hints to help you through.

Find a hiding place as far away from the noise as possible. For me, this usually meant heading down to the basement. I found a dark little corner under an old workbench that made the sounds almost impossible to hear, and there were no windows so I couldn't hear anything. So check around your house and see if you can find a place like that. But having said that, you should also know that these crazy things are usually short-lived. I've never seen any last more than a few minutes, even though it seems like a lifetime when you're a dog! And as scary as they may be, you aren't really in any danger. That's really all I have to say about fireworks. But thunderstorms, now that's a dog of another color!

I hate to admit it, being the old wise man that I am, but I am still afraid of thunderstorms. Even though these old tired ears hear very little of them anymore, there is still something heavy and frightening in the air that sets my every nerve on edge. And the lightening! It's more frightening than anything. The flashes are so bright and shoot down from the sky as if the world is going to end. I sense fear and anxiety in my people too, and that makes me even more afraid. My every instinct tells me to go to them and help them feel less afraid, and yet, my own soul is so terrified that all I want to do is run and hide. In the end, I just wind up pacing around the house until the whole thing is over. I usually find a dark spot not far from where my people are, and I go from there to them and back again. I have had several good friends over the years who have offered suggestions for overcoming their fear of storms, but none of them ever worked for me.

One fine chap, a Golden named Branson, used to wear quite a funny looking blanket that his folks called a storm coat. It was supposed to eliminate that scary feeling that fills the air, but my people somehow never got wind of this invention. It didn't look all that comfortable anyway.

Another friend, an old mongrel named Lad used to hide outside under the cars. I suppose maybe he felt safe there, but let me tell you, he didn't stay dry and I'm sure he could still hear all the thunder!

So, I'm sorry to say, friends that thunderstorms are just a part of life to be endured. With any luck, you'll only experience them once in a while. Trust in your people to take care of you and you'll be fine. Stick together always, for that is where your strength lies.

Rabbits and Groundhogs

Everyone always talks about dogs chasing cats. Well, I for one, have never bothered to chase cats. For one thing, I simply don't like their attitude, and for another, there are so many of them around, they are just simply of no interest to me. But show me a rabbit or a groundhog, and it's game on! Both of these creatures are fast and whenever our paths cross, it's like the green flag waving at a car race. I'm ready to chase them and they're ready to run.

At the house where we used to live, there was a place we all called the meadow. Like I said before, my people always made sure there was a place for me to run free wherever we lived, and this house was no exception. There wasn't a real "dog Park" like there was in the big city, but it was a spot where everyone who lived nearby brought their dogs. I think it was just a part of an old abandoned farm field but it sure was a great place to play.
 We weren't the only ones there, though. It was also the place that several groundhog families called home. Now these weren't just your everyday groundhogs, either. I'm pretty sure they were fans of the game I've heard of called "Whack-a-Mole." These crafty little devils would pop up out of their holes just high enough and long enough to catch our attention and then once we got close they'd duck down out of sight and leave us standing in the middle of the field looking all of lost and confused, like some kind of simpletons. After a while we caught on to their tricks but we never stopped chasing them. We liked to get all the new pups in the meadow to chase them too, so we older guys could sit back and have a good snicker at their foolish antics. Oh, the joys of being an old dog! Rabbits galore lived in this field as well. We chased them on occasion, too, but they didn't see it as a game quite like the groundhogs did. When we came upon a rabbit, they seemed to be genuinely afraid of us. I suppose that's because there are some of our kind who do chase and catch rabbits, just out of instinct. As for myself, I was purely curious about the little fellows. I wouldn't dream of ever hurting one, but I always thought they would offer up a great game of tag if they just had a little more trust. I often hear my people laughing and telling others about my foiled attempts to initiate a game of chase with a local family of rabbits. I was trotting along, nose to the ground, when I suddenly came upon a rabbit hole. I stuck my nose in and had a long sniff. There

was definitely somebody home! I drew back and waited by the hole. Sure enough, within a few seconds, a large rabbit stuck his head out. I jumped up, he took a look at me, and headed back down! This happened several times. Up, down. Up, down. I couldn't figure out what kind of game this was, but it kept me occupied for some time. Turns out, that was his game plan all along! While I was busy playing pop up with him, his family of little ones was escaping to safety out the back door. Karen and Will had been watching this whole comedy unfold and were quite amused. Of course, I had to act like I knew what had been going on all along so as not to lose any respect from the gang. Truth was, I had to give those rabbits a lot of credit. Pretty smart fellows, I'd say!

One day a rabbit and I had a great game of chase in our back yard. One morning when Karen first put me out, there was a small rabbit munching happily away on some plants in our garden. I was just a pup still, and I ran over to say hi, thinking he would want to play. As soon as he saw me he scooted to the fence without even so much as a sniff in my direction. Thinking he wanted to play tag, I chased after him. He beat me to the fence then turned and shot back across the lawn. Of course, for me, across the lawn was only a few strides, but my bunny friend was running his little legs off. We continued that game for some time. Up to the edge of the fence and back. Up to the fence and back. I was just deciding that this game was getting a bit boring when on one trip to the fence he suddenly disappeared through a little gap. He took off into the forest leaving me panting after him at the fence. Seems he wasn't playing tag with me after all, but was searching frantically for that escape route! Oh well, it was fun while it lasted!

Criminal Dog

Believe it or not, I have a criminal record. I'm not an aggressive dog by any means, but the laws in the city can often work against us when people fail to be a little understanding. Let me tell you about the one time I got Karen into big trouble with the courts.

We had all gone for a run at the dog park as we often do on sunny days. The three of us, myself, Tucker and Pirate, another family dog were all in the back of our SUV. We pulled into Tucker's driveway and got ready to jump out. The adults were busy getting all the kids out of the car and into the house so they just opened the back door and let us out. Just as the last of us got all fours on the ground, a lady appeared from around the corner of the fence walking her little sheltie. When he spied the lot of us he began tugging on his leash and barking, which naturally drew our attention. Since he was barking a big hello, we barked back and all ran over to greet him. I guess to his owner this seemed like an attack. Quick as a wink she snatched her little guy up into her arms and headed for home. Disappointed that we couldn't say hello, we all retreated into the house. Little did we know that she had been terrified by our approach and had called the police to report us as vicious and out of control.

Later that evening, an agent from the humane society, accompanied by a policeman came to Tucker's door to give him a ticket for being "at large" which I guess means running loose. On the following days, Pirate and I also received tickets from the humane society. Karen was really upset by this, claiming that we were on our own property and had not in fact done anything wrong. To her, and to all of us, it seemed just like one big over reaction by a very nervous lady. Kind of a "her word against ours" situation. After all, her dog started barking first. And all we wanted to do was say hello. But laws are laws, say the humans who write them, and technically we were off leash where we weren't allowed to be.

Even though Karen took the issue to court, stating that we were actually on private property and under complete control, she still had to pay the fine. That was my second strike. My first was much less traumatic for everyone, but it got put on my record just the same.

It all happened when I was still a very new adopted dog, a puppy still, and very nervous around everyone. Karen and Will had taken me out for a walk on my leash and had stopped to talk to some neighbors. Their little guy was buzzing all around us on a three wheeled riding thing called a "big wheel." It was low to the ground, and he kept zipping past my back end where I couldn't see what he was doing. I was getting really scared by the speed and the noise of the wheeled thing right behind me. One time he came just a little too close and I snapped my head around and snarled a warning. I had no intention of hurting him and I certainly didn't mean to bite him. But just as I snarled, he came a little too close, and I nipped his leg. He squealed and ran to his people. Will pulled me in closer on my lead and scolded me a bit, then made sure the little guy was ok. It seemed like a pretty superficial wound.

We continued on our walk, thinking the incident was forgotten, until a knock came to our door the next morning. Seems the boy's folks took him to the hospital to make sure the wound didn't require stitches. When they reported it as a dog bite, they had to tell them about me. Now there was an officer at our door making sure I had had all my shots and that I wasn't going to be a danger to anyone.

Will explained the whole situation, and I was given the ok to stay home. For a wee minute there though, I was really scared. I thought for sure I was headed back to the shelter once again. I've heard humans say something about three strikes and you're out. Well I'm not entirely sure what that means , or where you go when you're out but I know I don't want to find out! I had two strikes against me and that was enough!

Will must have read the fear in my eyes because after the agent left, he gave me a big hug around my neck, and told me not to worry. He said I was their dog now and nobody was ever going to take me away again. I gave him a very grateful lick, and vowed to trust that Will and Karen would keep me safe; Even from wild kids and noisy wheeled contraptions.

Bakery Dog

This will be a short chapter from the story of my life but it was full of good times so it is worth a mention. You see, for a while I was a business dog. Now, I wasn't the CEO of the company or anything, but I was the CTT. This stands for Chief Taste Tester. You see, Karen and Will owned a dog bakery. It was named after me and my cousin Tucker. It was called Tucker O'Riley's Dog Bakery. Let me tell you, it was a grand place for a dog to spend his days. Every day Karen baked fresh treats and dog food for her customers. There was every kind of dog treat you could imagine. There were cheese treats, chicken treats, bacon treats, birthday cakes, frozen doggie yogurt and tons of other tasty stuff.

Of course, it was my job to make sure everything met Karen's high quality standards before they hit the shelves. I can hear your drool hitting the floor! Ya, it was a tough job but some dog had to do it! Karen was always careful not to feed me too many treats though. She was always looking out for my health!

The dog bakery was a neat place to socialize too. You see, Karen allowed, even encouraged, her customers to bring their dogs into the bakery. I got to know some of the regulars pretty well and we had some good times together. Holidays were always the best. We had special events for Christmas and Halloween. At Christmas the dogs came in and helped their owners fill a stocking full of special treats. Everyone did a lot of gift shopping too so the shop was full of extra awesome squeaky toys and stuffies. There was such excitement in the air. It really made me feel good.

At Halloween believe it or not, we actually had costume parties! Now, I think these were definitely more for the benefit of the humans than the dogs. I mean, what dog really wants to parade around in a fireman's jacket or a pair of fairy wings? Well, I suppose some of the tiny little fluff balls that came in the bakery didn't mind, but it was sure painful for some of us bigger guys and gals. But, we love to please our masters, so we do it, right? And really, isn't it worth wearing some goofy get up if it means a few extra yummy treats?

We even played games at these events. Maybe you've heard of people bobbing for apples? Well we canine creatures like to bob for hot dogs! Go figure!!!!

Anyway, Karen ran the dog bakery for a few years and then it was time for us to move on again, so it was closed down. I must say, I was sad to see it go. Those were some good times. But all was not lost. Karen continued to cook the same yummy homemade food for me, and she still bakes fresh treats every week. No store bought milk bones for this guy! But listen up, friends. If you're ever on a road trip with your folks and you pass a sign for a dog bakery, make sure you get the word across that you want to stop in. I hear they are springing up all over the country, and they are well worth the visit!

Life in the Woods

Well we have moved once again. This time, we are living in the country so there is no longer the need to find leash free parks for this dog! Here I have three acres of my own woods to explore. There is a cool hiking trail right out our back door that Karen and I walk every day, morning and night. There are so many smells out there I never have time to sniff them all. Some of them get my neck hairs in a buzz but most of them are just interesting. I stay clear of ones that smell like skunk or bear, but I am curious about most of the others like deer, moose and chipmunks. I haven't encountered many of them face to face but I know they're there.

One night I felt a low growl just start all by itself in my throat. I felt a real need to warn my folks that something was not quite right outside. Will opened the door and I pushed myself against his leg trying to warn him to stay inside. He got out one of those fancy lights that shine from his hands and pointed it into the backyard. Sure enough, my fears were right. Right at the edge of our deck stood a black bear trying to get the bird seed Karen had left in the storage box. He had torn the lid right off and had the bag of seed in his teeth. Will banged on the door and the bear took his prize and ran off into the woods. No harm came to anyone, but I was on alert for the rest of the night, and the next day when we walked the trail. But I guess Mr. Bear had satisfied himself with his bird seed and had moved on. I know he is never very far away though because I can still sniff his scent. I keep my bear alert growl ready all the time just in case!

One of the other smells I have come to know is Moose. They are some big, let me say, and not an animal I want to get very close to. They don't ever come too close to the house, though, and they don't really represent a danger to my owners. I smell them around now and then but they pretty much go their way and let the rest of the world go by.

One other slight annoyance is the flies. There seems to be an abundance of these in the woods. First come the black flies in late May. They are tiny, pesky little devils that get in my ears and try to feast. Karen has a special spray that she douses me with. Trouble is, I don't much like the smell or the feel of the spray, but it beats getting all chewed up! Deer flies and horse flies are a nuisance too. They aren't nearly as stealth as the black flies. In fact, they're about as bold as it gets. They buzz all around my head and land right on my nose! I try to brush them off with my paws but sometimes they take a chunk out of me first! The big secret with those guys is to keep moving. They seem to have trouble getting a good hold on a moving target. But if you want to take in an afternoon snooze, it's best to do it inside!

All in all, I enjoy being a country dog. It is different than living in the city for sure. It's a lot quieter for one thing, and I don't have to worry about busy roads. I never have to be tied up or leashed and the freedom is absolutely wonderful. I have lots of spots where I can dig big holes if the urge strikes me, and there is a small stream I can muck around in to cool off. The water tastes pretty good too! There's tons of space to play Frisbee and more sticks just laying around than any dog could ever catch or chew. And the grass! This country place has lots of grass for munching. Now I don't know about all dogs, but I can tell you, there are few things in this world more tasty than a fresh young shoot of grass that's covered in morning dew. That is a treat to be savored! Yep, living in the country has been a blast. Or at least it was until last spring. That's when my life changed a lot.

Stink Eye

I am a one eyed dog. When people say I'm giving them the evil eye, or the stink eye, as they sometimes say, it is really the evil _eye_! I used to have two eyes but one day last spring I did a rather foolish thing and now I am forever more a one eyed dog.

It was middle of March, a beautiful spring day. There was still a lot of snow on the ground but it was starting to melt. It was hard knowing where to step to keep from sinking up to your belly. I'm getting on, you know, and dragging my hind end up out a snow drift is pretty hard work. This day, I should have been a little more careful where I walked.

I had been laying quietly enjoying some nice spring sunshine on a dry bit of deck when all of a sudden a group of chipmunks began to chatter. They were chasing each other all over the yard and making one mighty racket! At first I tried to ignore them, but then my chasing bug got the better of me and I took off after them. All caught up in the chase, I didn't pay attention to where I was going. I ran up onto what I thought was a pile of snow. Next thing I knew, the snow gave way and I was plunged into a pile of brush that had been buried. There was a lot of snapping and cracking and then all I remember is a lot of pain. I suddenly couldn't see out of one eye and my head felt like someone was jabbing me with a giant needle. I remember yelping and running for all I was worth to get away from whatever it was that was attacking me.

Eventually I heard Karen's voice coming to me through my fog of pain. I knew I had to go back to her for help. I followed her voice and found my way back. By this time the pain was dulling a bit, but I still couldn't see very well. I was panting like a locomotive, and my heart was still racing. Karen brought me inside and calmed me down. Karen made an emergency appointment for me and the doctor gave her lots of medicine. For the next couple of weeks I had to endure eye drops twice a day, and great big pills that Karen tried to disguise in slices of cheese. Karen thought she was pulling the wool over my eyes, but I'm too smart for that. I never let on that I knew the pills were in there. After all, cheese is one of my most favorite treats. As hard as it was, I tried my best to be a brave dog and take my medicine willingly. I could tell how sad it made Karen feel to have to give it to me, especially the eye drops. She would always say she was sorry. I wanted to make her feel better, tell her it wasn't her fault, and the only way I could do that was to take it all like the big dog I am.

By this time, the pain in my eye had become something like a dull, always just kind of there, headache. I could endure it, but I never felt really normal. I couldn't see anything out of my damaged eye, either, so life was a bit unpleasant. After several check-ups, the doctor told Karen and Will that my eye was not going to get any better. If they left the eye alone, it meant I would have chronic pain for the rest of my days, and there was also the risk of infection from the deceased eye. The alternative was to remove the eye. And because the doctor said that was the best choice for my health, that is what Will and Karen decided to do.

I remember the day we left the hospital after getting that news. I could tell Karen was feeling really down about it. I didn't know how to make her feel better so I just stayed real close by and sent her lots of dog love with my good eye. I was really wishing there was some way that I could tell her that life with one eye would be just fine. How frustrating not to have human language! Turns out, there was someone else who was going to pass that information along for me. We stopped at one of my favorite parks on the way home, and I will be eternally grateful that we did. As we pulled to a stop in the parking lot, a dog that was there with his owner came running over to the car waiting for me to get out and say hello. Karen was hesitant to let me out afraid that I was not yet up to playing with a rambunctious friend. As Karen got out of the car, the other lady apologized for her dog being so bold. Karen said it wasn't a problem, but that she just wasn't sure how much I would feel like playing. As Karen explained my condition, and the news we had just received, the other lady smiled and said that she'd like us to meet someone. She called over another of her dogs that was standing nearby. As he got closer, Karen and I realized that this fellow had no eyes! His owner explained how they had both been removed due to disease, and that he was living a happy, productive life even though blind. Karen and the woman chatted for a bit, and the blind dog and I got acquainted. By the end of our visit I knew Karen was feeling a lot better. I guess sometimes good things just happen when you really need them to!

The appointment for surgery was made for the following week. I felt really bad because the day they chose was Karen's birthday. She should have been out celebrating and having a good time. Instead she was sitting at home worrying about me. Anyway, it all went well and I was back home in my own bed by suppertime. I was so sleepy from all the drugs that I just slept for hours. By the next day I was feeling much better. Within a week my stitches had come out and I was free of pain and the headache that had been there since the accident was gone. I had to adjust to seeing with one eye, but that didn't take long. I still bump into things from time to time if I turn too quickly on my blind side, but all in all, I've done very well. One thing I do know for sure is, I won't go chasing any goofy chipmunks through the snow!

Senior Dog

Well it's been a year now since I became a one eyed dog. That happened when I was 11, and I have started to slow down a bit now. Life is a little harder with one eye, but I am still loved and cared for and give back as much love as I can. My ears have stopped working as they should, and I sometimes have trouble hearing what people are saying. I know Karen still smiles and gestures when we are heading out for walks or rides in the car, and I still understand that. I know that I don't always hear people when they call to me, and quite often people reach out and pet me before I even know they are close by. I get startled sometimes but I always know as long as I am with the people who love me, that I am safe.

I can't hear the chipmunks much anymore so there is less temptation to go chasing them. I'm also happily oblivious to most crashes and bangs of thunder. I still feel the air change when there is a storm, and I still get freaked out by the lightening, but the rumbling rolls of thunder that used to set my nerves on edge no longer bother me. Thank goodness for small mercies!

One thing I'm not any too happy about is the stiffness I am beginning to feel in my back end. It's such as effort now to get up after I've been napping. I don't run much anymore either. Try as I might, I just can't get these old legs going. I have given up chasing sticks and my Frisbees have all been retired to the toy box. They now form the substance of my dreams. Just stop by sometime and you'll find me blissfully napping with legs, eyes and jowls twitching in delight as I relive the antics of my youth.

I can't jump up onto the beds anymore, and that is really something I miss. There's just nothing like pulling all the covers that smell like your people into one big pile and snuggling in! But I can still make it up onto the couch, so I'm good there. I have my own thick bed, too, when I want it.

Getting in and out of the car is a challenge, but amazingly enough, there is always someone there to heft my mighty back end up if I need help. Road trips are still the best fun of all and I don't want to ever have to miss them! I sleep more now, but that is a privilege of the old in any species, and I take full advantage of my position.

All in all, I have had a good life. Even though things were a bit rocky in the beginning, and I will not likely ever completely forget those days, I have forgiven the people who gave me my first home. They did their best to love me, but ours just wasn't a good match. I am thankful that they had the kindness to take me where there was an opportunity for me to find new people to love me. I know it was probably hard for them to admit their failure as it was hard for me to admit that my love was not enough for them. But we have all moved on. I hope they have found a dog that is right for them because everyone should experience the kind of love that only a dog can give.

As for me, I will be forever grateful to Karen and Will, and to Codi, whose soul I believe is what brought us together. From that first day when I licked Karen's hand, to the final moment in the future when we look into each other's eyes for the last time, I will feel forever loved.

Back at the Park

I can hear the ruckus before I even get to the gate. "Here he comes! Riley is here! It's story time!" I pick up the pace a little, just to show that I can, ignoring the stiff hip joints that protest my vanity. I lift my head and wag my tail high. These young pups can really use a mentor to help them learn the ropes. That is my purpose, my aspiration. As I approach the gang, I study the crowd and decide what story I will tell today. Will it be a tale of courage and bravery? A tale of calamity and humor? Or maybe something a bit more touching for the girls. After all, even an old dog like me still likes to impress the ladies! Whatever story it ends up being, I know it will be good. For all my life has been good. I am a blessed dog, but right now, my audience awaits.

the end

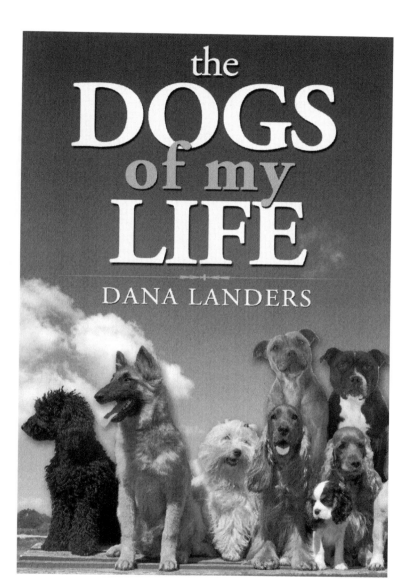

The Dogs of My Life

A Note from the Author

As I write this story, I am holding back tears. Not too long ago I had to say goodbye to my beloved Riley as he finally lost his battle with Degenerative Myelopathy, a nerve disease of the spine. I have been through the loss of a dog several times, but it never gets any easier. Those final moments play over and over in your mind, and each time your heart feels like it is being torn apart. Eventually, as the healing begins, you start to realize that this period of immense grief is really quite small when compared to the enormous amount of love, loyalty and companionship that you have received over the years.

But as with all pain, time is the best healer. Eventually you start to remember the good times, and when you do, if you're like me, you are left in awe of the power of the love of a dog. Their ability to give so much to us, in what is really a very short amount of time, is incredible. As I reflected on this recently, I realized that the periods of my life can easily be defined by the lives of the dogs that I have owned. From the days of a young newlywed couple, to the golden years of retirement, my husband and I, along with our children, have been blessed by the lives of 5 dogs of our own. Each one had a different story and each one had an enormous impact on our lives. This is their story. I write this for them, for the dogs of my life.

Shiloh: "The Newlywed Dog"

Shiloh was our first baby. Like many young newlywed couples, the
topic of having children was a frequent one. But, as was the custom
"back in the day" we decided to wait a little while. We followed the
advice of our elders and took a little time to "get used to each other
and to being married." But the urge to nest and start a family was
strong, so we decided to start our "family" anyway, and we got a
dog.

My husband had always wanted an Irish Setter, and when a friend
at work said he had a litter of pups ready to go, the die was cast.
We were having a baby! Shiloh was the only purebred dog we have
ever owned. He was gorgeous, with his sleek red coat and long
silky ears. But alas, it seemed he was not destined to be the
brightest crayon in the box! He couldn't seem to ever grasp even
the basic of commands. We would take him out one day to practice
his newly acquired skills and he would seem to be mastering things
just fine. Then we would walk him the next day and it was like
starting all over. We eventually gave up on any training other than
the basics, which pretty much amounted to him walking halfway
decently on a leash and not jumping up on people. (Most of the
time). He had a small bump on his head that is quite typical of his
breed. We lovingly referred to it as his bump of knowledge, and as
it was very small, well.....you get the picture.

Shiloh was the only dog we have ever owned that actually jumped
out of a car window. As all dogs do, he loved to ride with his head
out the window, and as first time dog owners, we thought it was
perfectly okay to allow it. We assumed dogs would know better
than to jump out of a moving vehicle, but we had overestimated his
intelligence once again. Fortunately, when it happened, we were
slowing down to park the car and he wasn't hurt. But it gave us a
scare, and I have never since been at ease with any dog having a
window down farther than just enough for his head to fit out. I
shudder and close my eyes when I see those great big pick-ups with

dogs riding in the back. I say a prayer for each of them that they stay safe.

As first time "parents" this dog was definitely a learning experience for us. We learned very quickly that a big dog in a small car meant lots of goobery face washes. There was just enough room between the front bucket seats for Shiloh to get his head and two front feet through, and that was his preferred method of travel when it was too cold to drive with the windows down. Unfortunately for us, he was also a very curious fellow which meant that his head swung from side to side as he watched the scenery roaring by. Each time his head went from left to right and back again, we were in turn bathed by the slobber that flew from those loose flapping jowls. I often gave thanks that I wasn't one to wear make-up because I would certainly have been a sight upon my arrival at any destination! As it was, we learned never to travel without a small towel in the glove box!

Like all children, Shiloh often helped us see the world through more innocent eyes. We routinely commented on his total amazement of the world around him. Everything he saw or encountered was a mystery to be solved, or a curiosity to be understood. One of the memories we have laughed about most often involved a road trip, a snowmobile and the wind. It was quite a blustery winter day and we were on the highway heading home from a family visit. In front of us, a truck was pulling a snowmobile on a small trailer. The wind was playing havoc with the trailer, swaying it from side to side and the movement immediately caught Shiloh's attention. For a while he was content to watch, his eyes and not his entire head (thankfully) following its movements. Then all of a sudden, as we followed a big curve in the road, things changed. The wind was now coming over the trailer getting under the black nylon cover of the snowmobile, causing it to billow and flap about. It must have appeared as some kind of threatening creature to Shiloh because he began to bark incessantly as he watched. In the small car, we were almost deafened by the sound, and had to pass the trailer or risk hearing loss. Shiloh quickly turned around as the monster fell back behind us, but soon lost interest as the distance increased. To this day we cannot pass a snowmobile on a trailer without thinking of him.

Unfortunately along with the many other ways that Shiloh was a first for us, he was also the first and only dog that we've ever had to give up. About a year into marriage, my husband took a new job in a city a fair distance away. We didn't have the funds to buy a house where we were going, and knew that renting would be in our future for a while. Back in those days, and I hate to say it, but even today, it seems most landlords are reluctant to allow pets, especially large dogs! The sad reality was that Shiloh would not be able to accompany us on our move. We had no family members who were in a position to take him either, so we were left to search for a suitable home for him on our own. The only thing we knew for certain was that we could not let him go to a shelter. He needed a good home with a loving and patient family, preferably with a lot of room to run. We were lucky to find that home in a friend that I had known from college. She and her family lived in the country and had room in their house and in their hearts for our large, loveable four footed child.

It was with many tears and guilt that we left our first dog behind that day, but it was also a lesson learned. I vowed then and there that no dog would ever come into our lives again that we couldn't keep, and I am happy to report that we have successfully kept that promise.

Captain: The Very First "Kids Dog"

My husband changed jobs several times over the next few years of
our marriage, and for that reason we had not yet taken in another
dog. We did have two "real" children, however within that time, a
daughter and a son. When they became old enough to start asking
about getting a dog, we were forced to take a close look at our
situation and make a decision. We felt pretty settled financially, and
had become homeowners. We knew that even if job changes
happened, we would be buying a home from this point forward.
And so it seemed like a good time to take that step.

We thought that perhaps, with two young children, a smaller dog
might be a good choice for us. We wanted the kids to have input
into the choice so one bright winter morning we all went off
together to the local shelter. Even though our first dog had been
purchased from a breeder, this time we wanted to give a home to a
dog in need of a second chance. I remember that there were very
few dogs in the shelter that day, but it didn't matter. A little black
bundle of wiry fur quickly worked its magic on both the kids and
us. The deal was sealed. Back in those days there was far less
paperwork and screening done for rescue dogs. We signed all the
necessary forms, paid the required fees and carried our new
bundle of joy home the same day.

The kids were in love with their new sibling. I can't quite
remember how his name was chosen, or who made the final
decision but he was named Captain. It was a pretty big name for
such a little scoundrel, but it somehow suited him. He would chase
them around, nipping at their heels and making them squeal at
every turn. We were never told what kind of dog he was, but the
wiry hair suggested terrier of some kind. But some other
mischievous breed was there as well because this little fellow was
quite the thief. Nothing was safe from his tiny little jaws. Things
that you would never suspect would often go missing only to turn
up in his bed or toy basket. His one true passion, however, was for

soothers, both those of his own siblings as well as visitors that came to call. We quickly got into the habit of having spares on hand for our own kids, but there was one time when a visiting niece of ours was not so well prepared.

Captain always had his soother radar on high alert, and when our niece dropped her soother on the floor after her nap, no one noticed except Captain. Quick and silent he was, and he stole away with the beloved rubber "nummy" without anyone even noticing. Much later that day, as the family was packing up to go home, our niece, tired and cranky after a long day of play with her cousins, demanded her "nummy" for the ride home. At first her mother looked in the diaper bag, the playpen, various pockets and pouches, all to no avail. Not knowing about Captain's little fetish, they didn't think to check the dog bed, the dog toy basket or the back yard. But we knew. And we checked all those places, also coming away empty handed.

By this time little Lindsey was screaming hysterically because there was no emergency nummy in their possession. I looked sternly at Captain who just stared back at me with a goofy look on his face. He was obviously going to guard his secret to the end. I tried to remember all the weird places I had found hidden objects before, which finally led me to the bathroom, and here I was finally successful. On several previous scavenger hunts I had found missing socks, missing toys and even missing kitchen utensils buried cleverly beneath the bathmat. And it was here that the much needed nummy was finally found. My sister never travelled anywhere ever again without a second nummy tucked safely away! It is truly amazing what life lessons can be learned from a dog!

As much as we loved Captain, ours was not to be the long and happy relationship that we had hoped for. He had only been our dog for a few short months when the unthinkable happened. It had been a very snowy winter and snow was banked high all along the roads, and especially at the end of driveways. On one beautiful sunny morning, I opened the side door to set some garbage in the carport. I didn't realize Captain was right at my heels as I did so, and he ran past me before I could stop him. Being the little devil that he was, he thought it marvelous to be running free, and was no doubt anticipating what he thought would be a fabulous chase. He barreled full tilt down the driveway as fast as his little legs could carry him.

As my heart started pounding faster, events started moving in slow motion. My eyes never left the blur of black fur as my peripheral vision caught the movement of an oncoming car. I knew they were going to collide, and I knew that little ball of fluff was no match for any car, even one going slow on snow packed roads. By this point I could no longer see Captain, and I could barely see the roof of the car over the snow banks. But I heard the sickening thud, and I saw the car pull to a stop just past the drive. With quick orders to the children to stay inside, I threw my feet into the first piece of footwear they came in contact with and ran outside. The driver was out of the car by this time and was kneeling over the still, quiet form that lay against the snow bank. I joined him there, resting my hand on the tiny body, hoping against hope that he might still be alive. I felt his heartbeat stop under my fingers as he let out his final breath. The kind driver asked if he wanted me to take the little guy somewhere, but I declined. He gave me a small blanket that he had in his car and we covered the body. Then with yet another apology he was on his way.

I returned to the house, worried that the children would come outside to find me. Only then did I realize I had run outside in my pajamas and housecoat and my husband's shoes! I called my husband who worked close by and he immediately came home to take Captain to the local animal hospital. The kids cried as they said good-bye and I cried once again for a dog we had loved and lost. We grieved for Captain, and eventually we were able to enjoy his memory and laugh at some of his crazy antics. But the children had now been touched by the love of a dog, and as all dog people know, once that happens, there's no going back. There would have to be another dog in our family.....and soon!

Marshal: "The Second "Little Kids Dog"

A few weeks later, we were back at the shelter again. This time, there were a number of dogs barking and fighting for our attention. My heart ached for all of them, and if I could have, I would have taken them all home. Our daughter was three at the time, and our son just over a year. He wasn't old enough to really have any input into choosing a dog; he was merely enjoying all the fuss and action. Out daughter, however was deliberating very extensively over the choices. She understood that only one dog was coming home with us, and she wanted to be sure, it was the right one. After spending the better part of a morning petting and talking to all the dogs there, she finally made her choice, and we had a new dog.

Again, I have no recollection of how the name was chosen, but this dog was to be Marshal. Thinking back, I wondered if my husband's love of TV police drama had somehow wormed its way into the decision making process. First a Captain and now a Marshal? At any rate, our daughter agreed, and Marshal it was.

Marshal will always be the dog I referred to as our first "Kids dog." The kids were at the perfect age to enjoy their new furry friend and they showered him with all the love and affection they could. In return, Marshal was patient and careful with them at all times. But as I watched their relationship unfold, I had a sense that it was somewhat one sided. Marshal never quite became the cuddle up in your lap, or lay on the bed beside you kind of dog. He was always gentle, and good to mind, but his heart always seemed to be somewhere else. As a rescue dog, details of his breeding were somewhat sketchy. We were pretty sure he had a fair bit of hound in him, and his determination to run off, as if in chase of some unseen prey, confirmed our suspicions. I always felt that, given a choice, he would gladly leave us behind if it meant he could hunt for his livelihood! But he was ours, and ours he stayed until the ripe old age of 14, and although he was never successful in getting his longed for freedom, it wasn't for lack of trying.

Before we finally moved to the "growing up" house, we lived in a small, semi-detached house in a large city. We fenced the yard right away so Marshal could finally be outdoors without being tied up. We hoped that this would be enough freedom to keep him happy and a little more settled. But try as we might, he was a determined fellow and insisted on digging holes under the fence as fast as we could fill them in. We tried adding lower boards to the fence but he had an uncanny talent for finding a spot where he could get under. One night while we were eating dinner, a knock came to the door. There stood our neighbor from up the street.

"You'd better come with me," he said to my husband. "I think I saw your dog lying on the side of the road. Looks like he may have been hit."

My husband seemed doubtful at first, certain that Marshal had been in the yard just before we sat down to eat. But as he pulled on a jacket, I checked the yard. Sure enough, our furry escape artist was gone. A few minutes later my husband returned carrying a frightened, but conscious Marshal in his arms. He had a long gash on the back of his head but seemed otherwise unharmed. After an emergency trip to the vet he returned with a shaved head, several stitches and a big plastic collar, which he absolutely despised!

But this was not to be his last attempt to gain freedom. A couple of years later, we moved to the house, as mentioned above, that we called the "growing up" house. We wanted the kids to stay in one place where they could make friends and settle into school. For Marshal, it meant a much bigger yard to run in, where we hoped he would finally be able to relax a bit. Once again, our hopes were dashed. There seemed to be no way to confine this dog! The yard was wide and completely fenced, but Marshal only ever made use of the back area along the fence. Every day, morning till night, if he was out in the yard, he would run, full tilt, from one end to the other and back again. He had a dirt track worn in the grass and he kept it well worn. At times, especially in the heat of summer, I would call him in just so he would be forced to rest. I couldn't help but feel bad that all he seemed to want out of life was to be set free!

We felt pretty confident that the fence around the yard was escape proof. The boards went completely to the ground, so he didn't attempt to dig underneath. I guess it was for that reason that we let our guard down a bit, which proved to be a big mistake.

I was inside doing a bit of cleaning one day, when, once again a neighbor tapped at the front door, this time with Marshal at her side. "I picked him up downtown" she said. "He was running down the middle of Main Street." Shaking my head at our wandering friend, I thanked her and brought him inside. With him safely behind closed doors, I went out to inspect the yard, certain that either the gate was open, or there was a big hole under the fence somewhere. As it turned out there was neither. This left the question of how our little Houdini had escaped. Eager to get to the bottom of the mystery, I decided to watch him closely the next time he was outside.

As always, he began by running back and forth along his trail. He didn't saunter either. He ran so fast that he kicked up a cloud of dust at each end when he turned around. I watched him for a half hour or so, almost convinced that his last escape had just been a fluke, that maybe one of the kids had accidentally let him out. I was about to give up my watch when I realized he hadn't turned to come back down his track. His running track ended in the far corner of the back yard that was hidden from view by our above ground pool. When I didn't see him return on his track I ran quickly to the edge of the pool deck to see what he was up to. Sure enough, he was repeating his escape plan from the day before. He was lying down completely on his side and was working his way between the basket woven fence boards. Now let me tell you, this was no easy feat! He was a medium sized dog and the gaps between the boards were pretty small. He had to put his head through and down and then work his body through. He was virtually turning himself into some sort of doggy pretzel. I clapped my hands loudly to get his attention. "Ahah! You've been busted!" I yelled. At the sound of my voice, he wound his way out of the fence and crept, head down toward the house. I couldn't believe the efforts he had gone to just to run free. We again did our best to fix the fence to keep him in, and for the next few years we had no incidents. He still burned up the dirt along the fence whenever he was out, but he didn't try to get out again.

But alas, being the humans that we are, we began to forget the past and let ourselves believe that our efforts had been successful. And, once again, he was to prove us wrong. The next time he got away, I was right there at home and still had no idea he had escaped. It was about four o'clock in the afternoon, and I was hanging out with the kids on the front porch. Other kids on the street were on their way home from school, and we turned when we heard their shouts as they approached our house. At first we weren't sure what they were saying, and then we saw Marshal running along in front of them. He seemed fine so we assumed the kids were just yelling to let us know that he was loose. But as he got closer, and turned into our driveway, it became quite apparent what all the fuss was about. Even though he was running home, Marshal had a huge deep gash that ran the entire length of his side. He was bleeding profusely, and to this day I don't know how he made it home. I wrapped him in a clean towel and off to the vet we went. The vet was also astonished at the fact that Marshal had been able to run home. The cut was deep and had lacerated some internal organs as well. But the vet said his prognosis was good, and he was right. This time he spent three days at the hospital to make sure he was okay and then he returned home once again stitched and collared.

By this time, Marshal was officially a senior dog. He had turned 11 the year of his big accident, and I guess by then he had grown tired of trying to get away. He could often be found trotting back and forth along his trail, as he never abandoned his efforts entirely. But he never again escaped the yard, and he drifted into old age accepting his captivity. When he was 12, the kids got anxious again to have a puppy. Knowing that Marshal would not be with us much longer, I agreed. I thought that having a pup around would help to ease the pain that comes with the loss of a beloved pet.

This time, the kids picked a furry little thing from the local pet store. He was only eight weeks old and as different from Marshal as he could be. The kids enjoyed their new companion, but I would often see one or the other of them sitting quietly and petting their old friend as he watched the new youngster bound around. They never ignored Marshal or forgot about him. He was loved, and in his own way, he loved us back. He finally succumbed to a brain tumor at the age of 14. My wish for him as I told him I loved him and said my final goodbye was that he finally get to that place he had been searching for all of his life. Our new friend Codi, did make the pain a little easier to bear, and as we grieved the loss of our "first little kids dog" we drifted easily into the next phase of our life.

Codi: "The Big Kids Dog"

The kids were old enough now not only to enjoy their new puppy, but were also old enough to take over some of the responsibility for his care. They took turns walking, feeding and playing with him so he never seemed to be more one child's dog than another. He was truly the "kids" dog. He was quite a bit smaller than Marshal and much more attached. He would bring chew toys to the kids to play tug with, and he did his best to learn a few tricks. They spent lots of time teaching him to sit, play dead and say please, all of which he would gladly do for a treat. But even with all of that said, this dog too, had some quirky ways about him.

Codi was always content in the yard that Marshal had spent his life trying to escape from. He showed no interest in following in Marshal's footsteps so eventually the grass began to grow back over the track along the fence. And while that part of the yard began to look better, other parts, the Codi parts, were starting to look even worse. Codi decided that he liked to lie in freshly dug garden soil, preferably in the shade of a large shrub. So needless to say, the mounded area under all of our bushes was completely dug away, which by any landscaping measure, was not a pretty sight. But that was his thing, and we had long ago learned that there was no hope in trying to stop or prevent it. Instead we lived with the holes, thankful at least that as long as he was lying in one of his spots, he was home and he was safe! To this day, those kinds of bushes are known as Codi bushes to all members of the family.

Just recently when our youngest daughter bought her first house, she asked me to accompany her to the nursery to buy some plants for her new garden. "I need you to help me pick out Codi bushes," she said. "I want some in my garden!" In fact, when the day came many years later to bury Codi's ashes, we did so in our big perennial garden, in the shade of a newly planted Codi bush dedicated to his memory!

All in all, Codi was a fairly calm dog. Other than barking at the mailman, he rarely made noise or caused any kind of disturbance. But he was terribly afraid of thunderstorms. Like most dogs, they would make him pace and fret, but I think his behavior was far more neurotic than most. At the first sign of a storm, he would start to pace from room to room, scratching at every door. He wouldn't rest until every closed door had been opened and left open. If you tried to ignore him, he would just keep scratching. To prevent all the doors from having the paint scratched off, we indulged him by opening every door. This meant that all closet doors had to stand open, along with the pantry door, the linen closet door, all bedroom doors and any inside access doors. Fortunately we had storm doors on the outside that we could leave closed without upsetting him. He did this every time there was a storm. Eventually, I began to simply go through the house and open all the doors at the first rumble of thunder. This seemed to lessen his anxiety somewhat, but he still paced until the storm had passed.

On one occasion during a storm, he managed to slip out into the yard when one of the kids ran out to grab some toys that were in danger of getting wet. Fortunately, he couldn't get out of the yard, but when he heard the thunder, he was too agitated to come back in. Instead, he wandered up onto our pool deck. Now, this wouldn't seem too strange unless you knew how much he hated the pool. The kids had taken him in once as a puppy and he had totally panicked. From that day foreyard he avoided the pool at all costs! So for him to even venture up there was most unusual, but the really weird part was that he decided to do a trick dog act while he was up there.

The pool was an above ground model, with decking on all sides but one. We left one side with just a flat wall against the pool, so there was nothing but the ledge of the pool along that side. This ledge was maybe about eight inched wide at the most. Now all of a sudden, here was our pudgy little ball of fur, up on the pool deck trying to walk along this tiny ledge. We all watched and held our breath, sure that he would end up in the pool at any moment. But this dog must have been a tight rope walker in another life because he made it all the way around to the larger part of the deck. In his storm induced panic, he headed back around the deck to do it all over again, but I intervened and grabbed him and brought him inside.

Our years with Codi flew by and it seemed in the blink of an eye his kids were all grown up. When we first brought that fluffy fur ball with the pudgy belly home, the kids seemed so young still. But somewhere along the way they had all become adults. Codi was there to see them all off into their busy lives as young adults. He watched each and every one of them go off to college, always waiting patiently for their return at holiday time. He saw each of them off into their first jobs away from home, and was there when our oldest daughter got married.

One day I realized that he had been at my side every time I cried over yet another departure from the nest. I remember coming home after my daughter's wedding and passing her empty room on my way to bed, Codi glued to my side in case I needed a furry shoulder to cry on. He sat with me on my son's bed the day after he moved his things out to take to his first new apartment, and he never missed a chance to climb in the car for the ride to pick up our youngest when she wanted to come home for a visit after she started a new job in a new town. Somewhere along the way, Codi had become just my dog, and he accepted his new role with complete devotion.

Also, during this time, my husband was still travelling a lot for work. Often when he was gone, there would just be the two of us, Codi and I, and I was always so grateful for his presence. He was a warm body to cuddle up with, a never tiring ear for all of my complaints and an ever eager companion for a walk. We bonded like we had never done when the kids were home, and it was wonderful for me. Having him there, lessened the impact of the kids leaving home, and for that I will always be grateful.

By this time Codi was 10, and although he was slowing down a bit, he didn't seem to be ailing at all. He was still eager for his walks every day, and he still jumped into the car for a ride every chance he got. But I did notice that he started having trouble getting up after he'd been lying down for a while. I put a lot of that down to his being overweight, and I tried to keep him active. And then one day, just out of the blue, everything changed.

I have told about Codi's passing in my first short story, Connected Souls, so I won't go into a lot of detail here. It was February of a very snowy winter. Codi and I had been for our usual morning walk, and then he settled down for a nap while I went to work in the lower part of the house where I did home daycare. Around noon, I let Codi out into the yard and he was fine. When I sent the last child home later that day, and came upstairs, Codi was lying in the middle of the living room floor. He made no move to come when I called him, and as I called to him I realized he was unable to get up. Codi never got up again.

The vet said he would never walk again, that there was irreparable damage to his spine, and that for quality of life purposes, it would be best to put him down. As hard as it was to make that call, we knew we had to do what was best for our loyal and loving companion. All of the kids came home to say their goodbyes and needless to say, it was a very emotional evening. Early the following morning, my husband and I said our last goodbyes to a friend we had loved for so long, and I have no shame in saying, that it was the hardest thing I have ever done. I cried all the rest of that day and for weeks to come, I would cry whenever I thought about him. Our nest was really empty now, and at times the loneliness was unbearable.

Then one day, I had an overwhelming sense that there was another dog out there who needed me. Although it seemed very soon after Codi's passing, I truly felt that the time was right to visit the local shelter. It was there that we met Riley. and I knew from first glance, that Riley was meant to be our dog.

Riley "Our Dog"

Riley wasn't riley when we met him, he was Cujo. Now, some people might have been put off by his name alone, without also considering his size, but when our eyes met and then he licked my hand ever so gently, our fates were sealed. He was coming home with us. For a split second I worried that I might be choosing him because he looked a bit like Codi. His coloring was similar, with a lot of black and brown, but that is as far as it went. Where Codi had been a small, spaniel border collie cross, Riley was a large, possibly shepherd, Bernese mountain dog cross. At eight months old he was already very tall and his large paws indicated that he was going to fill out even more. But it didn't matter. It was love at first sight. As I have written in my first story, I will always believe that the spirit of Codi led us to Riley and to a dog that would fill our hearts and our home with more love and companionship than we could ever imagine. Our nest was no longer empty.

All of the kids came home to meet their new sibling, and while they were glad I now had another dog in my life, they all expressed some concern about having such a big dog in my life. It wasn't long however, before his big heart won them over and they loved him for the gentle giant that he was.

The first order of business, of course was to change his name. My husband suggested Riley from the old TV show "The Life of Riley." It was a phrase that had become synonymous with having a great life, and that was exactly what was in store for this dog. We were aware that he had been treated poorly by his previous owners, so we were determined that his life would be good from here on. And so Riley it was!

There were some behaviors that it took Riley a little time to get over, but with love and patience, he soon learned to relax and trust us. Once that happened, he became the most loyal and loving companion. He remained cautious of strangers, especially men for a long time, but as long as folks just gave him a chance to come to them at his own pace, he was fine. He was always gentle with kids, and we believe he must have come from a family where there had been children. As our children began to have families of their own, Riley was always there to watch over his young charges. They could pet him, crawl on him, pull his fur and he would never complain. Even when he was old, deaf and half blind, he still welcomed their attentions.

During the first years that Riley was with us, I was still doing home daycare and my husband was still travelling for work. It was always a comfort to look into his big brown eyes at the end of the day and know that I was never alone. I was convinced that Riley never really had a sense of his own size because he truly believed he was a lap dog, even though his head alone would fill my lap! If one of us sat on the couch, he would jump up and place his entire front half right across our laps and lie down. He wouldn't stay long because I'm sure he was most uncomfortable, but he always held out long enough to have a good scratch.

Time seemed to fly by over the next few years, and since Riley's arrival we had stopped thinking about him being our empty nest dog, and started calling him our "golden years dog." Somehow, with the arrival of grandchildren, our nest was seldom empty anyway! There was always someone coming for a visit!

We were seniors now, and Riley was right there growing old along with us. He kept us active at a time when we might have been more inclined to be lazy and that was a good thing for us. He was still chasing a Frisbee up until the age of nine, when it started to bother his teeth. At that point we started throwing sticks that he would fetch and bring back. He was still fetching sticks at the ripe old age of eleven, until an accident in the snow cost him an eye. After that, he could no longer track the path of a stick through the air, so we settled for simple walks in the park.

About a year or so after losing his eye, we realized that Riley was also losing his hearing. It was sad to watch this happen, but it never dampened his enthusiasm for life. Where I used to only have to whisper any of his favorite words like walk, park, or car ride to have him up and at the ready, I now had to use a sign language of sorts. I could tap my leg to indicate walk time, or wave my car keys in the air and he knew it was time for a ride. Where before a simple "You can come," would answer the ever present question in his eyes as we prepared for an outing, I found I now had to nod vigorously or shake my head slowly to let him know whether or not he was to be included in the excursion. We also had to make some concessions to his loss of one eye. We had to keep pathways clear of items he could trip over, and we tried to avoid rearranging furniture so he wouldn't bump into things. All in all, he compensated very well, and never lost his easy going nature.

By the age of 12 he was beginning to signs of arthritis, and this was confirmed by our vet at his regular checkup. He took his vitamin supplements like a trooper and they seemed to really help for a while. He was definitely slowing down though, and we noticed him doing less and less of the things that he loved to do. He could no longer jump up onto our bed, where he often loved to nap in the sunshine. He had a lot of trouble getting in and out of the car, and needed a boost from behind most of the time. He would slip on the wood flooring that covered our entire house, so we laid a pathway of rubber backed mats from room to room. His appetite began to decrease, even for his favorite foods, and this seemed to signal the beginning of more serious issues.

At a check up for his arthritis, our vet suggested an x-ray to rule out the possibility of a tumor that might be causing his difficulty of movement. Fortunately, there was no tumor, but the doctor did confirm that Riley was in the advanced stages of Degenerative Myelopathy, which meant there was a lot of nerve damage to his back end. This explained his difficulty with getting up and his dragging of his back leg. At times, especially on uneven ground, his back end would simply give out. We were now giving him pain medication each day to make him comfortable and to help him get around, but we watched with sadness as his condition worsened. There was nothing more we could do for him except love him and care for him, which we did with every ounce of our souls. I often felt I wasn't doing enough in return for all he had given us, but it was all I could do. We watched him carefully for signs that it was time to let him go, knowing that he would try to please us as long as he thought we needed him to. When he could no longer remain on his feet long enough to relieve himself, we became very concerned.

Then the day came when he just didn't try to get up any more. He would look at the door, or look at his water dish, but then lie his head back down. He was tired, and in pain from his arthritis. The DM had advanced to a stage where he could no longer get up on his own, and we knew it was time. He was almost 13 by now, and for a big dog, that is considered a long life. But if you've ever loved a dog then you know that even 13 years is not long enough.

Unfortunately, there is no way to end this story on a happy note, as it is ending with the loss of a very dear friend and companion, and quite possibly our last dog. We are older now, and wonder if we would be able to give a dog the outings and exercise that it deserves. I worry at this stage, that a new dog might even outlive us, and feel then feel abandoned by the owners who once loved him. But I am also finding it hard to live without the unconditional love and companionship that only a dog can give.

It would seem that for now at least, with the passing of Riley, our nest is really empty. Will it remain that way? At this point, I can't answer that. The pain of losing Riley is still too fresh. But time is the great healer, and with time, who knows? Like I said at the beginning of this story.....once you've been touched by the love of a dog it's awfully hard to live without one!

The End

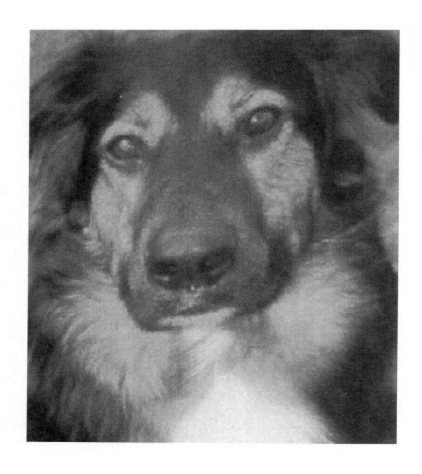

In Loving Memory of Riley

2000-2013

For Riley

There's an empty space here on the couch
Where you would share my fears
There's an empty space here in my lap
Where your fur would catch my tears
There's an empty space beside my bed
Where you slept by my side

There's an empty space in the cars back seat
Where once you loved to ride
There's a quiet stillness in the park
Where once you ran so free
There's a great big hole here in my heart
Where my dog used to be

--Dana Landers

Thank you for purchasing this book. I hope that reading it has inspired you to hug your dog a little more, or remember with love, a dog that has touched your life. I hope it has also made you smile. I love to connect with my readers to hear how dogs have made a difference in their lives.

You can write me at danalandersbooks@gmail.com.

If you can spare a few moments, I would also appreciate a review on this book. You can leave it on the book's sales page on Amazon.

Thanks for reading!

Printed in Great Britain
by Amazon